A SOUND APPROACH TO
TEACHING INSTRUMENTALISTS

A Sound Approach to Teaching Instrumentalists

An Application of Content and Learning Sequences

●

STANLEY L. SCHLEUTER

The Kent State University Press

Autography by A. C. Vinci

2 2o5 2 9

Copyright© 1984 by Stanley L. Schleuter
All rights reserved
Library of Congress Catalog Number: 83-26771
ISBN: 0-87338-298-6
Manufactured in the United States of America

Library of Congress Cataloging in Publication Data

Schleuter, Stanley L.
  A sound approach to teaching instrumentalists.

  Includes bibliographies and index.
  1. Instrumental music--Instruction and study.
I. Title.
MT170.S34   1984   785'.07   83-26771
ISBN 0-87338-298-6

To Lois, Monika, and Scott

CONTENTS

FIGURES

PREFACE

INSTRUMENTAL music is an important force in the musical culture of this country. Thousands of children learn to play instruments in our schools every year, but many instrumental teachers, because of training or instructional philosophy, attend primarily to the technical skills of instrumental performance. School instrumental music programs often become characterized by more attention to group performance levels than to individual musical development. The result is that school instrumental music programs are often criticized because a majority of instrumentalists lack musical independence and, in many cases, musicianship.

What is this book about? This book examines the application of musical content and learning sequences to teaching instrumental music to students from elementary school through adult ages. A basic premise is that music consists primarily of tonal and rhythmic content and that instrumental teaching and learning can best be accomplished through expression of musical content and ideas. Teachers are encouraged to have open minds and to be eclectic in their choice of materials and techniques. Efficient learning and teaching can occur when musical content and learning skills are properly sequenced. The aim of the approach described in this book is to meet individual student needs and differences of musical achievement.

This book supplies material that is usually omitted from "comprehensive" texts for instrumental music education classes. The book's content is concerned with teaching tonal and rhythmic understandings while developing instrumental technique. The aim is to develop students who have something to perform rather than students who just perform something. Such specific technical information as fingering charts, bowings, embouchure formation, or hand positions for various instruments are intentionally omitted from this book. Nor does this book include discussions on how to organize a music library, prepare for a trip, prepare a budget, and so on. This information is widely available in many other sources.

The book is organized into six chapters. Chapter 1 is a brief chronology of teaching instrumental music in the schools of this country. Major influences upon development of school instrumental music programs are discussed. Chapter 2 provides contributions of selected psychologists and educators, with current knowledge about learning processes as a proposed basis for teaching instrumental music. Developing a sense of tonality and a tonal pattern vocabulary is discussed in chapter 3, which includes tonal content sequence and teaching techniques. A list of tonal objectives in a sequence of learning is provided. Chapter 4 deals with the concept of developing a sense of rhythmic feeling and a rhythm pattern vocabulary. Rhythm readiness, content sequence, and teaching techniques are also discussed. A list of rhythm objectives in a sequence of learning is provided. How to acquire instrumental skills while learning tonal and rhythm pattern vocabularies is explained in chapter 5. Learning sequence is used as a basis for diagnosing musical problems and arriving at solutions, and lesson examples are included. Finally, chapter 6 provides measurement techniques for tonal, rhythmic, and instrument skill objectives. The chapter deals with standardized tests and describes techniques for reporting instrumental achievement.

Who should read this book? This book should be of help to anyone who plans to teach or currently teaches instrumentalists. Studio teachers of private lessons will also benefit although most of the discussions refer to teaching beginning instrumentalists in school settings. The book is appropriate for undergraduate and graduate instrumental music majors, studio teachers, and especially for school music teachers.

How can this book help you? Your efficiency as a teacher should be improved by following the sequences for tonal and rhythmic content. You should be able to organize musical objectives as a basis for teaching instruments and meeting the needs of individual students. Your skills in diagnosing problems and prescribing solutions should improve. Most of all, your students should become more musical and independent as instrumentalists.

Teaching will not necessarily become easier as you improve your diagnostic and prescriptive skills. Instead, the process increases in complexity The demands on the teacher for flexibility and conceptualizing of musical content, materials, and teaching techniques will increase. You will no longer be satisfied with requiring all students to do the same thing at the same time or simply to follow the page chronology of an instruction book. The end result, however, will be the increasing rewards of developing musically functional student instrumentalists who gradually become independent of their music teachers.

1

AN OVERVIEW OF PAST AND CURRENT PRACTICES

THE TEACHING of instrumental music in the schools of this country is a relatively recent phenomenon. School instrumental instruction began in the mid-1800s and was not widespread until after World War I. The rapid growth in numbers of students currently involved in school instrumental music programs is a tribute to many dedicated music teachers of the past seventy years. How and what students have been taught has also shown growth and development over the years as their needs and expectations have evolved.

Until the late 1800s, music teaching in our schools consisted mainly of vocal instruction. Private teachers provided instrument instruction through individual lessons conducted outside of public school settings, the most popular instrument being the piano. Teachers, instrumental teaching methods, and materials frequently originated in Europe. Birge [1] lists four reasons for the increased impetus of school music instruction that occurred during the last half of the nineteenth century: 1) the growing influence and professional recognition of private music teachers, 2) the proliferation of choral groups and festivals, 3) the formation of professional symphony orchestras and professional bands, and 4) the establishment of college music courses and music conservatories.

In addition, community bands and orchestras gained in popularity during the late 1800s and influenced public support for school groups. Outdoor band concerts in parks became a popular form of entertainment, and bands were often formed by town governments, industry, and colleges but rarely by public schools. Band members had to study their instruments with private teachers. An example of the thinking of the period comes from the 1880 edition of *McCosh's Guide for Amateur Brass Bands:*

> While the study of music educates the mind, it helps to purify and refine the character . . . the most practical way of indulging a taste for the arts, is in the organization of brass band . . . . A Brass Band, it is true, in its commencement, may be termed a noisy organization, but all music was evolved from the chaos of sound by the discovering mind of man . . . . So it will be after a time with a Band. Its members will learn to master their instruments, and blow gentle notes of sweet melodies, instead of the harsh sounds that come from inexperienced lips. Thus, through the energy of perseverance, a lovely result may follow. [2]

School orchestras and bands were established intermittently between 1850 and the end of the century in states from Kansas to Massachusetts. Instrumentations of school bands and orchestras were diverse. Bands often contained various stringed instruments, and orchestras might include any instruments available. Groups were often made up of no more than ten to twelve members. Students continued to learn how to play instruments from private teachers, and group rehearsals usually were held outside of regular school hours.

School instrumental programs were accepted slowly during the last half of the nineteenth century, but several key events helped promote the need and desire for teaching instruments in schools. First, instrumentalists from military bands of the Civil War became available as teachers. After the war, bandsmen scattered across the country and served as conductors of school or community groups in addition to private teaching. Second, musical instruments had developed technologically, and more of them began to be manufactured in this country. The Boehm system was introduced on clarinets and flutes. The saxophone family gained in popularity. Piston valves became the standard on brass instruments. Third, professional orchestras and bands began to standardize instrumentations. Between 1842 and 1900, professional orchestras were formed in New York, Boston, Chicago, St. Louis, Cincinnati, and Philadelphia. It was during this period that the bands of Patrick Gilmore and John Philip Sousa gained international reputations. Fourth, the phenomenal growth in numbers of public high schools (from about 100 in 1860 to about 6,000 by 1900) provided settings for future instruction of instruments. Finally, John Dewey's "learn by doing" philosophy of education began to have a wide influence in school curricula, by diminishing the classical orientation of curricula and encouraging students to participate and experience in order to learn.

Major Influences in the 1900s

Four major factors continued the spread of instrumental music instruction in the schools during the first three decades of this century. The first of these was World War I. Service bands were used extensively to entertain troops and to rally patriotism, and the federal government became a large and important market outlet for instrument manufacturers. Following the war, many bandsmen and conductors became music teachers in the schools, and the music instrument industry actively worked to develop school music as a new marketplace. From the 1920s on, more and more school orchestras and bands were formed that rehearsed during the school day, were financed by school funds, and were directed by a full-time school music teacher.

The second major influence was the formation in 1907 of the Music Supervisors' National Conference, later to become the Music Educators' National Conference (MENC) in 1934. Although mainly concerned with vocal music in the early years, by the 1920s and 1930s, this organization served to promote school instrumental music across the country through publicity, teacher conventions, and teacher training clinics. Outstanding school instrumental organizations performed at many of the conventions and did much to convince teachers and school administrators of the potential for school instrumental music. The Committee on Instrumental Affairs had impact nationally by recommending instrumentation standards, publishing lists of literature, disseminating teaching methods and ideas, and organizing competitions.

The third major influence on the growing numbers of school instrumentalists was the national contest movement. The School Band Contest of America was organized in 1923 by instrument manufacturers as a promotional device. In the same year, the Committee on Instrumental Affairs of the Music Supervisors' National Conference took control of the contest and reorganized the rules and format, with the first national school band contest occurring in 1926 and the first national school orchestra contest following in 1929. The contests grew in popularity each year until they ended with the 1940 competitions. The contest activities helped delimit the instrumentation of school bands and orchestras, and directed more attention to providing appropriate music for school groups. Thousands of students from all over the country participated in the competitions and represented their schools and communities. The numbers of school instrumental teachers and the quality of instruction grew accordingly, and public support for school instrumental music reached new heights.

The fourth and perhaps the most important influence upon the proliferation of school instrumental music was the development of class instruction techniques and materials. Free class lessons in schools were the key to involving the masses of students needed to complete the growing instrumentations of the orchestras and bands. Class lesson techniques became the mass production device for instrumental music. As class lessons were introduced, grade school bands and orchestras became commonplace and served as training grounds and "feeders" for high school performance groups.

Class Methods

The first widespread instrument class instruction in this country was for classes of violins. Charles Farnsworth visited England in 1908 and observed that hundreds of thousands of English children were being taught violin by class instruction. Albert Mitchell, after learning of Farnsworth's discovery, visited England in 1910 to study the class lesson techniques. After returning to this country and experimenting with the process, Mitchell developed and published the Class Method for Violin. [3] It was later adapted for other instruments. The Instrumental Music Course by Benjamin Stuber was another violin class method published at about the same time. [4] New techniques for teaching and managing class groups of instrumentalists continued to evolve rapidly during the 1920s and 1930s; the reference list at the end of this chapter provides additional sources of detail on these methods.

Teaching classes of mixed instrumentations received great impetus from Joseph Maddy and Thaddeus Giddings with the publication of The Universal Teacher in 1923. [5] This material permitted even more flexibility with heterogeneous groups of instruments. The method emphasized melodic rather than technical drill material. Students were also expected to sing the melodies and transpose by ear, and harmonizations of some melodies were also included.

Class instrumental instruction became predominant soon after the dissemination of usable instructional materials in schools. Although private lessons also continued in many schools, class instruction was considered by many to have more advantages. Theodore Norman discussed five such advantages:

1. It opens the way to all children to discover their talent and interest in music by offering instruction at little or no cost . . .
2. Class instruction socializes the music lesson by encouraging cooperation, self reliance, and good sportsmanship . . .
3. The mortality is lower because of the increased opportunities to stimulate and maintain interest . . .
4. Class teaching permits and encourages a rich and extensive musicianship by correlating previous music study in the schoolroom with ear-training, design, sight-reading, ensemble-playing, and the like . . .
5. Class instruction enables the director to develop and maintain a symphonic instrumentation. From the class group the director can choose according to the needs of his organization . . . . [6]

Method Book Content

The two types of class methods (like or mixed instruments) have continued to the present day. Method books also continued to be published for individual lessons. Most individual instrument method books contained a majority of technical drill exercises and very little material of melodic interest. Class methods are currently the reverse and use a majority of melodic material.

Drill and technique material was generally emphasized in like-instrument methods such as the *Rubank Elementary Method* [7] in contrast to heterogeneous class methods. Exercises are mainly brief studies emphasizing chords, scales, rhythms, articulations, and fingering technique. Others, such as the *Smith-Yoder-Bachman Ensemble Band Method,* included mostly short melodies for the purpose of technique development. [8]

Fingering charts and occasional pictures of embouchure, hand positions, and posture were included in most early materials designed for class instruction. Content of later publications followed similar formats.

Rhythmic content is the underlying organizer in nearly all instrument method books. Almost all authors organize their material around proportionality of note values beginning with whole notes and rests, then progress through half, quarter, and sixteenth notes and rests. Mathematical and visual connotations of note values are stressed. The basic rhythmic difference among the various methods is the pacing of new materials and the amount of material presented which emphasizes each note value. Various counting systems are included (1-e-and-a most common) and are always simultaneously introduced with the notation. If any correlated physical movement is advocated, it is usually foot-tapping. Assumptions are made that students do not have or need rhythm readiness activities prior to beginning with music notation.

Most methods contain no directed material or information for developing a sense of tonality. Most melodies are in major mode and, especially in more recent books, are limited to a few keys. Arpeggio and chord studies are usually intended as fingering or articulation exercises rather than as tonality training material. Inclusion of much melodic material does indirectly aid the development of a sense of tonality.

Between 1940 and about 1970, a number of new class method books were published; their content, however, was basically variations of the method books from the previous twenty years. A few innovations in content appeared during the 1970s. Some method books such as *Take One* by Charles Peters and Matt Betton contain material in jazz idioms. [9] *The Individualized Instructor* by James Froseth systematically approaches rhythm training without using the proportional note value approach. [10] It also makes extensive use of melodic rounds and includes the words with familiar songs.

Most instrumental class methods that appeared over the past half century emphasize: 1) the association of fingerings with notation, 2) the mathematics of proportional note values, 3) note naming, and 4) a mixture of technical and melodic material. There has been little or no concern with correlating materials or techniques with classroom general music content beyond the coincidence of some common songs.

Other Developments

A number of other developments have enhanced or changed teaching techniques and materials during the past fifty years of school instrumental music training programs. Colleges and universities have established elaborate degree programs and requirements for instrumental music education students. Courses of study typically include instruction in teaching techniques, materials, and instrument skills in addition to music theory, music history, applied instrument study, and general studies.

Marching bands, concert bands, jazz ensembles, and symphony orchestras are commonly found in colleges and universities. These organizations often approach or reach professional levels of proficiency and become models for high school groups. Instrumentations, performance styles, and compositions and arrangements are directly influenced by college performance groups.

State teacher certification requirements now permit only music graduates with certification to teach in public schools. State requirements often determine undergraduate curricula. The number of instrumental music teachers available for school positions has continually increased.

Available repertoire for teaching instrumentalists has grown considerably in quantity and quality. Publishers of method books often have a catalog of supplementary materials ranging from beginning to advanced levels. The materials include solos for all instruments, small and large ensemble collections, technical drills, and selections for full band or orchestra. Composers and arrangers have capitalized on the needs of school instrumentalists. Newly composed music in a variety of styles is available for all instruments and groups.

The main emphasis in school instrumental music programs continues to be large performance groups, particularly at the secondary level. Participation in grade school and junior high school groups is often considered as preparatory training for participation in high school groups. Class lessons in many schools are primarily concerned with preparing the music for the band or orchestra. There has been much criticism of overemphasis on performing groups.

Many instrumental teachers are now being held accountable for achievement of musical objectives by the individual students in addition to the accomplishments of group performance. In addition to preparing selections for the next concert, rehearsals may include such activities as directed listening, analysis, composition, and arranging.

At the junior and senior high school levels, many schools also stress availability of instrumental learning opportunities for any student who wishes to participate rather than offering groups for only a select few. The most common school instrumental groups, orchestras, bands, and marching bands, are established as early as the elementary grades; marching bands have become increasingly popular because of their public visibility in parades, festivals, and football shows. These groups often become the main display unit of school instrumental music programs. Although the emphasis in marching bands should be upon musical development, they are often criticized for ignoring musical objectives.

Stage bands or jazz ensembles also continue to increase in popularity in both junior and senior high schools. The inclusion of a style of music that incorporates improvisation is appealing to many students while allowing for musical objectives to be stressed.

Small ensemble activity may also be found in many schools at all levels. Solo and ensemble contests often act as a stimulus for the formation of small ensembles. Guy Kinney and other writers emphasize that small ensemble performance is an excellent method to develop musicianship and instrumental technique.[11]

Recruitment of beginning instrumentalists has always been an important part of school instrumental music programs. Much has been written about recommended procedures. Instrument manufacturers provide free advice and materials along with promotional "tests." The National Association of Band Instrument Manufacturers (NABIM) published a pamphlet in 1974 which offers information and suggestions.[12] Procedures have been refined with the publishing of legitimate music aptitude tests and with research studies concerning improved efficiency of beginning instruction procedures.

The fact that the majority of instrumentalists who graduate from high school do not continue playing their instruments is a subject of concern for music educators. Opportunities for adults to participate in community bands and orchestras are minimal. Raymond Roth attributes the dearth of adult amateur bands to four factors:

> 1.   As directors of school bands we have devoted so much energy to our own groups, that we have not been able to provide the leadership or expertise needed in developing successful amateur adult bands.
> 2.   In some instances competition has been emphasized so strongly to our school students that musicality and the love of music has been lost. They want out.
> 3.   In some instances school instruction has been so poor that students want no further exercises in mediocrity. Real musicianship was never developed.
> 4.   We do not have one effective professional band organization to address the issue. Individual groups have attempted to create a central organization, but there has not been any coordinated effort. [13]

It is also possible that adult instrumental participation would be more prevalent if more small ensemble and chamber music experience were emphasized in school curricula. Desire for continued instrumental experience by adults must be built upon musicianship experiences in school years.

Research Efforts

Modern research and development by instrument manufacturers has resulted in better quality instruments of all types. Acoustical research has aided in determination of effective design. With current technology, instruments are mass produced with micro-tolerances in mechanism and uniform ease of playing. Instruments of high quality are manufactured so that even student-line models are reasonably priced. Schools and beginning instrumentalists can afford instruments that play well in tune, are easy to maintain, and are widely available.

Research efforts continue to provide information and suggest how the teaching of instrumentalists may be improved. Doctoral dissertations have made a significant contribution and such bibliographies as the *Woodwind Research Guide* by Lyle C. Merriman [14] give the teacher and researcher an indication of the extent of available information. Two 1972 publications by the MENC are also of particular interest: *Teaching Performing Groups* by Charles H. Benner and *Teaching Instrumental Music* by George L. Duerksen. [15] Both booklets provide research syntheses relating to instrumental instruction.

Perhaps the most important research relative to instrumental teaching is that concerned with how music is most efficiently and effectively learned, a topic receiving increasing interest both at the research and the developmental levels. The results often confirm or question the effectiveness of many of the traditional techniques and methods, and new techniques and sequences are suggested as improved teaching strategies. The remainder of this book is primarily concerned with how instrumental music teaching and learning may be improved through application of much of what is currently known about how music is learned.

Review Questions

1. What was the status of school instrumental music prior to 1850 in this country?

2. What were some of the events which helped proliferate school bands and orchestras during the last half of the nineteenth century?

3. What were some of the major influences upon school instrumental music during the early 1900s?

4. Discuss the beginnings of class lesson materials.

5. What is the basis of content organization of most instrumental method books?

6. What are some of the more recent developments which have contributed to continued growth of school instrumental music?

7. How have research efforts affected school instrumental music teaching?

8. Considering the past 150 years, what do you foresee as the future of school instrumental music instruction?

For Further Reading

Colwell, Richard J. *The Teaching of Instrumental Music.* New York: Appleton-Century-Crofts, 1969.

Fennell, Frederick. *Time and the Winds.* Kenosha: Leblanc Publications, Inc., 1954.

Green, Elizabeth. *Teaching Stringed Instruments in Classes.* Englewood Cliffs: Prentice-Hall, Inc., 1966.

Holz, Emil A. and Roger E. Jacobi. *Teaching Band Instruments to Beginners.* Englewood Cliffs: Prentice-Hall, Inc., 1966.

Prescott, Gerald R. and Lawrence W. Chidester. *Getting Results with School Bands.* New York: Carl Fischer, Inc. and Minneapolis: Paul A. Schmitt Music Co., 1938.

2

THE PROCESS OF LEARNING MUSIC

American music educators traditionally have been advocates of getting things done, be it vocal and instrumental instruction or just philosophizing about the objectives of music education. They have not, however, been equally alert to possible improvements in music instruction suggested by the findings of research in the psychology of learning. To an extent, the upshot of this situation has been an unintentional neglect of both important factual data and learning theory in favor of more or less traditional methods of instruction. As a consequence, the instructional program in many instances has lacked the direction which learning theory can provide. Theory and practice have not always been in agreement.[1]

IN THE twenty-five years since Louis P. Thorpe made this observation, much has been learned and published about the process of learning. The application of this knowledge to music learning is only the beginning. Most instrumental music teachers teach the way they were taught as children; they seldom examine or question traditional methods and techniques of instruction with regard to current theories and knowledge about music learning. Good, bad, and inefficient methods and techniques of teaching music persist through unquestioned adherence to tradition.

How music is learned and how it should be taught has been the subject of scrutiny by some music educators and learning theorists. Most of what is written is personal opinion based upon experiences in teaching music. Some is based upon general psychological principles applied to music learning. Only a small amount is based upon experimental research. Perhaps the overriding cause for inefficient music teaching is music teachers who lack skills in diagnosis and prescription of musical and instrumental problems. Instead of diagnostic proficiency we find perpetual trial and error. By forgetting and/or ignoring what is known to be efficient techniques for teaching instrumental music, teachers often substitute reliance on materials in the order printed in "method" books. Music instruction under such circumstances becomes simply a series of favorite techniques that keep students occupied, working, and sometimes learning.

Rather than attempting to relate a history of learning theories, the discussion in this chapter will center around contributions of selected psychologists, music educators, and researchers who have provided important ideas for improvement of music teaching and learning. Those chosen for inclusion are well known for their impact upon education and music teaching. It is interesting to note the degree of commonality among their theories and how the theories relate to the practice of music teaching. It is beyond the scope of this book to cover the entire field of learning theories. Selected references for further reading and study are included at the end of the chapter.

Psychologists, Educators, and Music Learning

Johann Heinrich Pestalozzi (1746-1827) was a Swiss educator-philosopher-psychologist whose ideas and practices have had considerable influence upon general education and school music teaching in this country. He believed the purpose of education was the development of the whole person rather than individual skills: integrating the moral, physical, and mental faculties produced a well-rounded individual. Learning was facilitated by the inductive method, which included three steps: 1) Concepts must be taught by experiencing whole objects, pictures, or things before names or symbols are associated. Learning occurs by moving from the known to the unknown. 2) After experiencing the whole, its parts are analyzed and then labeled. 3) The parts of the whole are synthesized, and the concept is considered as an abstract. Pestalozzi's ideas first became popular in Europe and then spread to this country in the early 1800s. Lowell Mason is credited with adapting much of the process to teaching music reading in Boston during the 1830s. Various adaptations of Mason's techniques continued to the end of the nineteenth century.

A psychologist who influenced many music teachers during the first half of this century was James Mursell (1893-1963). For over thirty years his writings covered topics of school music objectives, curriculum, implementation techniques, measurement, and psychology of music. Mursell and Glenn wrote *The Psychology of School Music Teaching* in 1931 with the stated aim "to bring together all the findings of psychological research which bear on the work of the school music teacher, and to show how they can help in dealing with the practical problems to be faced."[2] Many of the points made in the book have remained valid through the years while other points are now outmoded by clearer understandings of learning processes.

Three of Mursell's basic tenets which remain current and valid are: 1) technique should be an outgrowth of musical expression, 2) familiarity with musical sounds should precede music reading, and 3) music should be taught in a cyclical sequence. The three principles are particularly appropriate to teaching instrumental music.

Mursell built a strong case for teaching musical skills and techniques through the demands of music. He was determined that musical expression should be the goal for technique development. Technical skills should be a means to an end rather than the goal itself; musicianship should be of primary importance.

Mursell also advocated the necessity for teaching music reading so that students could understand and manipulate musical concepts. Learning to read music should be the result of immediate musical experiences. "They [symbols] must be taught always in terms of their musical meanings and in application to musical situations and experiences, never merely in terms of verbal definitions and arithmetical designations."[3] This approach is directly related to Pestalozzi's thinking that concepts should be experienced before labels and symbols are applied.

Based upon his understanding of human growth and development, Mursell, in his later years, proposed that music content should be taught in a cyclical sequence. "In a cyclical sequence, the various items that need to be presented do not occur once for all at some predetermined time. They appear again and again, always in new settings, always with added meanings."[4] This conceptualization of learning has been supported by other psychologists and has influenced many school curricula. The application of cyclical process to teaching music is appropriate; however, a problem still exists when the sequence of music content has not been efficiently or logically determined.

The thinking and writings of Jerome Bruner have had considerable impact upon public school education processes during the past twenty years. In *The Process of Education*, Bruner develops four main topics: 1) the role of the structure in learning, 2) readiness for learning, 3) the nature of intuition, and 4) motivation to learn. [5] His discussions are not specific to teaching any particular subject content and may be generalized to music teaching. Bruner states that "the curriculum of a subject should be determined by the most fundamental understanding that can be achieved of the underlying principles that give structure to that subject."[6] Comprehension and recall are possible when fundamentals are understood and details are presented within structured patterns. As subject matter is structured and comprehended, transfer of learning to unfamiliar situations also becomes possible.

Bruner explains his concept of readiness as "the proposition that the foundations of any subject may be taught to anybody at any age in some form." [7] This means that children of differing age levels and adults could learn the fundamentals of music if presented in an appropriate form. Bruner supports the contention that children pass through various stages of intellectual development, and that learning tasks and content should be appropriate for whatever their level. He also declares that learning a subject content involves three processes—acquisition of new material, transformation of knowledge to fit unfamiliar circumstances, and evaluation of the appropriateness of the transformation. A series of episodes, each including the three processes, builds the knowledge of a subject matter.

The term "spiral curriculum" is used by Bruner to explain how fundamentals of a subject matter gradually expand in depth and complexity as the learner proceeds through various grade levels and continues to study and apply the same concepts. This is similar to Mursell's "cyclical sequence." In order for the concept of readiness to be operational in a music curriculum, it would be essential for the content and learning process to be carefully sequenced with continuity through all grade levels.

Bruner advocates that education should include the training of intuitive thinking; intuition, he explains, involves immediate apprehension of a "whole." In music, intuitive thinking could be fostered through such activites as composing, arranging, and improvising. This process of arriving at conclusions without prior analysis is not emphasized in much of our current music teaching.

Bruner's final point is that the willingness or motivation to learn is most effective when based upon what is to be accomplished. For example, when students enjoy performing music on an instrument and expressing themselves musically, they are more motivated to continue receiving instruction and to practice performance skills.

In *Toward a Theory of Instruction*, Bruner states that a theory of instruction for a subject content must be prescriptive and normative. An instructional theory must be based upon effective experiences, efficient structure of knowledge, sequence of content, and pacing of rewards for learning. All of these concerns are a necessary part of teaching instrumental music. Sequencing musical content is of particular interest in the succeeding chapters of this book. Bruner states:

> Instruction consists of leading the learner through a sequence of statements and restatements of a problem or body of knowledge that increases the learner's ability to grasp, transform, and transfer what he is learning. In short, the sequence in which a learner encounters materials within a domain of knowledge affects the difficulty he will have in achieving mastery. [8]

The psychologist Robert Gagne has influenced many music educators with his hierarchy of "conditions" or levels of learning. [9] Gagne divided the learning process into four basic perceptual levels—Signal Learning, Stimulus-Response Learning, Chaining, and Verbal Association; and four basic conceptual levels—Multiple-Discrimination Learning, Concept Learning, Principle Learning, and Problem Solving. Gagne's learning conditions provide a structure for sequencing learning processes and subject content. The levels of learning are a series of prerequisites for understanding the concepts which comprise a subject matter. Edwin Gordon first discussed the application of Gagne's classifications of learning to music education.[10] Later, Robert Sidnell provided music content examples for each of the eight levels. [11]

Benjamin S. Bloom and his associates have recently completed an extensive study (Development of Talent Research Project) of over 120 individuals who exhibited the highest levels of accomplishment in the arts, cognitive fields, or athletics before reaching age thirty-five. The study was intended to provide information about how we learn and fulfill our potentials. Among the subjects studied was a group of highly accomplished young concert pianists. Bloom and Sosniak compared talent development and school experiences and stated, "In general, school learning emphasizes group learning and the subject or skills to be learned. Talent development typically emphasizes the individual and his or her progress in a particular activity."[12] They further point out the role of home support in learning: "In general, where the school teaches the same subject or skill that parents emphasize, learning is likely to be very great—unless there are conflicts between the home and the teacher about the way to teach it." [13]

Other generalizations from the Bloom study include: support, attention, and rewards from teachers and family were critical at all points; all subjects of the study began instruction at an early age and took at least ten years of work to reach high levels of accomplishment; learning and instruction progressed in phases with each phase a prerequisite to the next. All of those studied were dedicated, hard workers. Bloom also mentioned that the children spent as much time on their talent development as other children spend in television viewing.

It can be generalized from Bloom's results that the musical talents of students can be furthered by school music teachers who analyze their own teaching procedures and content and improve their teaching skills. Parent support for beginning instrumentalists is necessary for early and continued success. The importance of knowing how to learn and how to teach music effectively should not be underestimated.

Generalizing from Psychology to Music

Through the years, efforts have been made by a few music teachers to apply the thinking of psychologists and educators to music instruction. One of the earliest examples is the influence of the Swiss educator Pestalozzi upon Lowell Mason. Mason adapted many Pestalozzian principles to music education in Boston during the 1830s and urged teachers:

1. To teach sounds before signs and to make the child learn to sing before he learns the written notes or their names;
2. To lead him to observe by hearing and imitating sounds, their resemblances and differences, their agreeable and disagreeable effect, instead of explaining these things to him—in a word, to make active instead of passive in learning;
3. To teach but one thing at a time—rhythm, melody, and expression to be taught and practiced separately, before the child is called to the difficult task of attending to all at once;
4. In making him practice each step of each of these divisions, until he is master of it, before passing to the next;
5. In giving the principles and theory after the practice, and as induction from it;

6. In analyzing and practicing the elements of articulate sound in order to apply them to music, and

7. In having the names of the notes correspond to those used in instrumental music. [14]

Mason put into practice a whole-part-whole method for learning to read music through singing. Music was experienced by singing and then analyzed, read, and conceptualized.

More recently, Emil Holz and Roger Jacobi listed five basic principles of instrumental class instruction. The principles are of interest because they directly reflect Mason's applications of Pestalozzian principles and are quoted here with some abbreviation:

1. . . . learning is often most effective when experience precedes theory, or in Pestalozzian terms, the thing before the sign.

2. . . . the teacher must organize instruction in such a way as to proceed from the known to the unknown.

3. The learning process proceeds most effectively when it is organized in such a way that the specific is related to the general and the general to the specific—in other words, from the whole to the parts and back again.

4. Throughout the educational process the teacher must realize that the important activity in the classroom is not teaching but learning, and that learning depends upon the desire to learn.

5. . . . teaching is the art of making students want to learn. In the beginning instrumental music class, then, teaching is not conducting, not lecturing, not judging. Teaching is motivating, explaining, demonstrating, encouraging, suggesting, organizing, and evaluating. [15]

The field of psychology has provided many insights into the general learning process, and much may be generalized to music learning. Research by psychologists has resulted in many areas of consensus about how learning occurs. It is generally accepted that the learning process is much more complex than early researchers believed. Moving from the known to the unknown is a basic tenet, but a sequence of prerequisites appears to exist within both the "known" and "unknown" stages.

Some conclusions we can make from the works of those theorists discussed and others are most useful to music learning: 1) Memory functions with short-term and long-term effects and involves the encoding and retrieval of information through organizing, classifying, and manipulating. Learning a vocabulary of rhythm and tonal patterns facilitates remembering music and becoming functional with composition and improvisation. 2) Frequent review activity is probably more efficient than drill for reinforcing new concepts and skills. Building upon previously learned musical skills is enhanced by review activities which keep earlier learning current and usable. 3) Complex tasks are learned by properly sequencing the content and following the prerequisite steps. Much less is known about prerequisites in music learning when compared to what is known and practiced in the teaching of mathematics or reading. Teaching and learning gain efficiency when prerequisites are carefully sequenced. 4) Tasks must be of appropriate difficulty to avoid undue frustration or loss of interest. This is particularly important when teaching music to young students. 5) Diagnostic and prescriptive teaching is possible when effective content and learning sequences are followed. This is a key factor in meeting individual learner needs and for becoming an efficient teacher. 6) It is possible to make the teacher dispensable by learning how to learn. A primary goal of teaching should be to help students become self-sufficient learners. 7) Active participation improves chances for learning to occur. Learning music is enhanced through demonstrating musical performance skills. 8) Learning is easier when the content is put to immediate use. Success in learning breeds further success.

Many music educators have begun to pay closer attention to research in psychology. Selected psychologists and music educators have held two symposiums (with a third planned) in an attempt to gain mutual understanding and to stimulate research, and papers of the first two meetings have been published as the *Documentary Report of the Ann Arbor Symposium*. [16]

Sequencing Music Learning

In traditional instrumental music instruction, a basic assumption is that repetition is of prime importance. The philosophy is that the more repetition, the more learning and retention. Teaching students "how to practice" usually means training them to repeat problem spots until errors are somehow corrected. Little attention has been given to the development of efficient sequences of musical content and learning processes with instrumental teaching.

Gordon has developed a sequence for learning music through tonal and rhythmic patterns.[17] Based upon Gagne's conditions of learning and also related to Pestalozzian principles, the Gordon music learning sequence has five levels of discrimination (perceptual) learning: Aural/Oral, Verbal Association, Partial Synthesis, Symbolic Association, and Composite Synthesis; and three levels of inference (conceptual) learning: Generalization, Creativity/Improvisation, and Theoretical Understanding. Discrimination levels are mainly concerned with the taking in of information or perceiving. Discrimination occurs with the familiar and known. Inference levels are concerned with the transfer and manipulation of information, or conceiving. Inference occurs when working with the unfamiliar and unknown. A musical vocabulary of tonal and rhythm patterns is acquired through the sequence and may then be performed instrumentally. Each of the levels can be summarized as follows:

Aural/Oral (A/O) is rote learning of tones through singing and of rhythm through experiencing movement responses to music. Listening to music and imitating the sounds of tonal and rhythmic patterns are basic to beginning music learning.

Verbal Association (VA) consists of the attachment of syllable labels (such as movable *do*) to patterns of sound. Word labels are also used for classifications and categories such as major, minor, duple, and triple. The verbal encoding of tonal and rhythmic pattern sounds with syllables facilitates their classification, memory, retrieval and synthesis.

Partial Synthesis (PS) is the beginning of musical syntax through aural combinations of patterns or recognizing learned patterns in familiar music without notation. Synthesis involves the connecting of familiar vocabulary patterns into familiar larger structures. It also involves developing aural recognition of tonality and meter of familiar music.

Symbolic Association (SA) involves attachment of music notation to familiar pattern vocabulary. This must involve both reading and writing music symbols after the previous levels of discrimination are accomplished for any given vocabulary pattern.

Composite Synthesis (CS) is the development of music syntax through visually recognizing patterns in notation of familiar music. Recognition involves audiating the sounds of the music notation.

Generalization (G) is the first level of inference learning and requires using familiar vocabulary to comprehend the unfamiliar; it is thus the moving from the known to the unknown. Generalization occurs when familiar vocabulary patterns are recognized in unfamiliar music. It is possible to spiral to Generalization from A/O, VA, or SA levels. Sightreading is Generalization at the SA level.

Creativity/Improvisation (C/I) occurs when familiar vocabulary is manipulated to improvise or compose variations or new compositions. It is possible to spiral to Creativity/Improvisation when preceded by Generalization at the A/O, VA, and SA levels.

Theoretical Understanding (TU) includes explanations of why things occur as they do in music, for example, intervallic relationships, scale construction, note proportionalities, and so on. Music theory information is of little functional use until music content has moved through all previous levels of the sequence.

A unique feature of the preceding sequence is the Verbal Association level. Tonal and rhythm syllables are aurally associated with sounds of specific patterns rather than with the notation of patterns. The syllables, in effect, become the "words" for remembering and manipulating familiar patterns before notation is introduced. Syllable systems have been used by music teachers for many years but in nearly all cases have been initially associated with music notation rather than sound. This is especially true in instrumental instruction. Without a verbal association stage, students must learn music by first listening to the sounds and then moving directly to notation. Although a necessary prerequisite, informal music listening in itself is inadequate without a verbal association stage. Unfortunately, many instrumental music teachers even omit the listening stage and begin exclusively with music notation.

The Gordon music learning sequence facilitates prescriptive and diagnostic teaching. The level of students' music achievement may be assessed and the next step prescribed according to the sequence. Learners should progress cumulatively through the five discrimination and three inference levels in sequence with the exception of spiralling activities as indicated in the inference level descriptions. If a student is unable to read certain patterns in notation, it would be appropriate to return to more instruction at the A/O, VA, and PS levels before proceeding again with reading activities. Prerequisites of discrimination levels must be accomplished before inference tasks of generalization, creativity/improvisation, and theoretical understanding become meaningful and appropriate. Students should have frequent opportunities for inference learning as new vocabulary is acquired in discrimination levels.

The sequence of skills for learning music is basically the same regardless of the age of the learner. The main difference in working with young children compared to older children or adults is the pacing and choice of materials and techniques. Younger children generally need more time with aural/oral activities. Older children and adults may often move more rapidly into music notation and are more analytical as beginning music learners.

Language and Music Learning

A useful analogy to learning sequence in music is the process by which we acquire language facility as children. Learning to read and comprehend language has many corollaries to learning to read and comprehend music. Acquiring verbal skills is mainly dependent upon the ability to hear and discriminate sounds. Acquiring musical skills and understanding is also mainly dependent upon the ability to hear and discriminate sounds.

If every paragraph you read first had to be rote-taught to you, you would be a very inefficient reader, would not read much material, would gain little or no meaning from the symbols by yourself, and would have great difficulty transfering your reading skills to unfamiliar materials. We do not expect children to learn to speak without first hearing speech. In addition, children gain vocabulary and verbal facility over a long time period through speech alone and without a symbol system.

Children learn to talk and later read through first hearing language. Eventually, they begin verbal expression and communication by imitating sounds of simple words for familiar objects (e.g., milk, food, cup, foot, hand, etc.) or for actions (e.g., run, walk, play, hold, see, etc.). Syntax is gradually developed through chaining words together into phrases and sentences. First language efforts are often used for expressing needs and feelings (e.g., Want drink!). Initial reading efforts involve seeing symbols for familiar spoken words and associating sounds and meanings. It is highly recommended that when beginning to read, learners hear words read to them by others. It is also important for beginning readers to learn to write familiar spoken words. Writing compositions with familiar vocabulary is also encouraged. While reading begins, spoken vocabulary continues to expand. Gradually, reading independence is gained for the vocabulary of words known (heard and understood) and then, the ability to generalize to the unfamiliar is possible. Spoken vocabulary is larger than reading or writing vocabulary during the initial years of learning to read. Lastly, children learn the theory of language, i.e., grammar, parts of speech, sentence structure, and so on.

Music learning should follow the same basic sequence of events for language learning. Music must first be heard and experienced (A/O) over a long time period. Aural familiarity is gained with listening to and experiencing simple melodies and rhythms. Tonal and rhythmic patterns should gradually receive syllable associations without notation and become meaningful entities (VA, PS). Symbols (notation) are then systematically introduced to represent familiar patterns (SA, CS). Unfamiliar music may then be learned and manipulated on the basis of what is known and familiar (G, C/I, TU).

Application of language models of learning to instrumental music instruction has been of interest to jazz educators because jazz performance demands improvisation facility, and improvisation skills may be acquired through first acquiring a vocabulary of tonal and rhythm patterns. The following is an aural-imitative method suggested for jazz pedagogy by Barry Velleman, a linguist:

- Ear training should precede music reading, and music reading should precede transcription.
- Class time should be used primarily for drilling improvisational patterns, usually without reference to written materials.
- Assignments should consist of the memorization of solo passages in addition to the preparation of class exercises.
- Explanation and theorization should be given less importance than the actual playing of patterns.
- As the lessons proceed, the instructor's cues should become less specific and contain progressively fewer elements of the desired student response. [18]

Velleman also emphasizes the necessity for students to model patterns of sounds after hearing the instructor. Terminology is then associated with the sounds rather than the symbols.

Learning and Instrumental Music

Instrumental music could be taught exclusively through rote training of songs and melodies. Many jazz and popular music performers, for example, do not read music. However, instrumental performers who do read music have a vast amount of solo and ensemble music literature available to them. It is much more efficient to perform on instruments when music reading skills are developed. A primary purpose for development of efficient music learning sequences is to produce functional musicians with music reading skills.

It is assumed that beginning instrumentalists in school music programs should read music. Unfortunately, most students do not read music when beginning on an instrument so they are given the instrument and a music book and are expected to learn music reading concurrently with the instrument. This is somewhat like learning to read as you learn to talk. Music readiness must occur first so that students have something to express musically with instruments and only then does notation take on musical connotations.

When beginning instrumentalists do not have prerequisite music reading skills, it is best to begin by singing and performing without written music. The teacher should emphasize that the instrument is merely a means to demonstrate and express what the student knows musically. Consider how accomplished jazz performers who are musically illiterate developed instrumental skills. The technique of the instrument was acquired to express musical ideas, not learned for its own sake with a forced application of musical expression added later.

Some instrumental music instructors speak negatively about rote training and believe that students fail to learn music reading when rote taught. These instructors do not understand or recognize the importance of initial rote training of songs and pattern vocabularies and the process of verbal association which then leads to music reading.

Many problems occur in instrumental music instruction because of the common practice of beginning with the symbols rather than the sounds and omitting enough aural/oral practice and efficient verbal association of patterns. Students are mainly expected to learn the technical skills of instruments while associating fingerings with music notation. By skipping the musical readiness for notation, music symbols become visual cues for fingerings rather than for musical sounds. Instrument performance becomes analogous to typewriting material without understanding the language.

Much remains to be ascertained about how music is learned. It is quite possible that more than one efficient learning sequence may exist. The level of learners' music aptitude may interact with various sequences of content or learning. High aptitude students may learn somewhat differently from low aptitude students. Individual differences may be accommodated in various ways. Without a doubt, learning music and performing musically on instruments are complex tasks.

The following three chapters are concerned with the application of learning sequence to instrumental music teaching. Tonal and rhythmic content and teaching techniques are approached through logical sequences. Instrumental technique is accomplished through musical content. All of the psychologists and educators discussed in this chapter have contributed to the approaches used; however, much of the structure and terminology is influenced by the writings of Edwin Gordon. In addition, the knowledgeable reader will recognize many of the same teaching techniques popularized in music education approaches by Shinichi Suzuki, Carl Orff, Emile-Jacques Dalcroze, and Zoltan Kodaly. A basic difference is the systematic and sequential application of the teaching techniques within a learning sequence structure. The materials and techniques which are advocated have been successfully field tested by the author and his students.

Review Questions

1. What is a major cause of ineffective instrumental music teaching?
2. How did Pestalozzi's ideas influence music teaching?
3. What basic tenets of Mursell are especially applicable to instrumental music teaching?
4. What is Bruner's concept of "readiness"?
5. How does Mursell's cyclical sequence compare with Bruner's spiral curriculum?
6. What are some of the current areas of consensus about how learning occurs?
7. What do the ideas of Pestalozzi, Mursell, Bruner, Gagne, and Gordon have in common?
8. What is unique about Gordon's Learning Sequence?
9. How does language learning parallel Gordon's Learning Sequence?
10. What is the role of Verbal Association in music learning?
11. What is the role of rote training in music learning?
12. When is it appropriate to introduce music notation?

For Further Reading

Ausubel, David. *The Psychology of Meaningful Verbal Learning.* New York: Grune & Stratton, 1963.

Hilgard, Ernest L. and G. H. Bower. *Theories of Learning.* New York: Appleton-Century-Crofts, 1974.

Woodruff, Asahel. *Basic Concepts of Teaching.* San Francisco: Chandler Publishing, 1960.

3

TEACHING A SENSE OF TONALITY

MOST traditional teaching of beginning instrumentalists excludes a developmental sequence for establishing a sense of tonality. (This is also true of many elementary general music programs.) Traditionally, emphasis is placed upon technical skills on the instruments, rhythm reading skills, and association of fingerings with notation. Instrumentalists are often preoccupied with reading pitch notation at beginning stages of learning. Reading from note to note with appropriate fingerings does not efficiently develop a sense of tonality. Instrumental students are allowed and encouraged to use instruments as tonal crutches by primarily associating notation with correct fingerings—not the correct sound. As a result, there are scores of instrument performers who "can't play without their music" and in fact, can't play with their music. Students need directed training to develop a tonality sense which will in turn greatly aid their instrumental performance. Instrumentalists should first audiate tonally and then compare the sounds produced on the instrument with that internalized model.

Defining a Sense of Tonality

A sense of tonality is an important syntactical device in nearly all Western music. It is a "glue" that provides continuity and expectation in the music of our culture. Both Robert Lundin and Paul Farnsworth discuss the cultural basis of tonality in music and its subjective development in Western music over many centuries. [1]

A sense of tonality is a learned phenomenon and requires tonal memory. Jack Taylor examined the tonality strength (degree of perception of tonal center) in short melodies by utilizing information theory and concluded that perception of tonality is learned. [2] In music, one remembers what he has heard and then anticipates on the basis of that which has become familiar. What is "known" is initially developed informally through listening to various types of music, often from radio, television, and tape or disc recordings. Understanding and expectation are enhanced by perception of tonality in music. Leonard Meyer has written extensively on expectation in music and how musical expectation aids understanding and organization. [3]

A sense of tonality is in effect a sense of mode. Modes are based upon various scale structures which are arrangements of whole and half-steps. Although other connotations may be found, for our purposes tonality is synonomous with mode. Aural recognition of major, minor, or other tonalities results from ease of perception of the tonal center of melodies and from chordal accompaniment. The resting tone (also called home tone, key tone, tonic note) is the tonal center for a given mode and is frequently the last tone of a melody. The two most common modes in Western music are major and minor. Songs occur with much less frequency in dorian, phrygian, lydian, and mixolydian modes. Of course, not all music in our culture has obvious resting tones to suggest specific tonalities. Composers of atonal and aleatoric music intentionally avoid feeling for tonal centers. The music used for beginning levels of singing and playing instruments is decidedly tonal in nature. It is generally agreed in practice that tonal music is taught and learned before other types are attempted.

Tonality should not be confused with keyality—the key letter name. Keyality is labeling a pitch perceived as the resting tone regardless of mode. Key signatures must vary accordingly. "The key of A" is not a meaningful statement unless the mode is also named—A lydian, A dorian, A major, and so on. Key signatures by themselves do not indicate either the mode or the key name of a particular selection until the resting tone is identified. Authors of beginning instrumental method books often ignore or misunderstand this important consideration. Instrumental music selections are sometimes notated with incorrect key signatures. A typical example is a piece in D dorian given the key signature of D minor (one flat) with all B-flats given natural signs throughout the piece. Another commonly found example is a tune in major mode with the resting tone of G notated with no key signature. A key signature of four sharps is appropriate for E major, F-sharp dorian, G-sharp phrygian, A lydian, B mixolydian, and C-sharp minor (see Figure 3.1 for the various possibilities).

Any tonality or mode may have as its resting tone any of the twelve chromatic scale pitches. Key modulations within a melody occur when the tonal center shifts to a different pitch level. When an entire melody is assigned to a new pitch level (new resting tone pitch), but the mode remains the same, it is commonly called transposition. Playing tunes at different pitch levels is greatly facilitated by a strong sense of tonality.

For instrumental students and teachers, some examples of demonstrating a sense of tonality include:

—knowing when a played or sung pitch sounds right or wrong; whether or not the pitch "fits" with the pitches around it

—aurally recognizing the difference among songs in major or in minor mode

—anticipating the resting tone of a tune

—aurally recognizing the cadential sections of a piece

—experiencing tonal audiation, i.e. "hearing in your head" what the next pitches should be before they are sounded

—knowing the difference between playing through a piece to "see what it sounds like" and knowing how it should sound before playing it

—functioning tonally with musically trained ears, eyes, and fingers.

Conversely, a sense of tonality is not:

—matching instrument fingerings with written notes

—knowing the names of lines and spaces on the staff

—reading, spelling, and playing scales

—memorizing that major scales have half-steps between the third and fourth and the seventh and eighth scale degrees

—knowing how to spell chords

—recognizing the key name of a selection by its key signature.

Research specific to instrumental music teaching and a sense of tonality is relatively sparse. Selected references are included throughout the remainder of this chapter with the intention of synthesizing research implications for instrumental music teaching.

Mode	Tonic Syllable															
Major	Do	C♭	G♭	D♭	A♭	E♭	B♭	F	C	G	D	A	E	B	F♯	C♯
Dorian	Re	D♭	A♭	E♭	B♭	F	C	G	D	A	E	B	F♯	C♯	G♯	D♯
Phrygian	Mi	E♭	B♭	F	C	G	D	A	E	B	F♯	C♯	G♯	D♯	A♯	E♯
Lydian	Fa	F♭	C♭	G♭	D♭	A♭	E♭	B♭	F	C	G	D	A	E	B	F♯
Mixolydian	Sol	G♭	D♭	A♭	E♭	B♭	F	C	G	D	A	E	B	F♯	C♯	G♯
Minor	La	A♭	E♭	B♭	F	C	G	D	A	E	B	F♯	C♯	G♯	D♯	A♯

Fig. 3.1.   Key and mode names for key signatures.

Tonal Readiness

Beginning instrumentalists should be expected to have some aural concept of tonality. These tonal concepts result from exposure since childhood to recorded and live music performances, and perhaps some contribution from classroom general music. Most of the music that children have heard is in major tonality, and thus their aural concepts of other modes are more limited.

Extensive singing is probably the most important activity for development of a sense of tonality and instrument readiness. In earliest childhood, children should be expected and encouraged to sing. Simple tunes and melodies with words should be learned by rote. Singing along with recordings of children's songs (preferably sung in tune by children) is a helpful activity. Parents should sing regularly to and with their children.

Beginning instrumentalists may or may not have a repertoire of familiar songs that they can sing, so that they may need to learn additional songs with singing prior to instrumental experience and continue to learn new songs while studying an instrument. Lessons and rehearsals should frequently include singing activities.

It is important to recognize that unless physically disabled, anyone can sing. Singing is an acquired skill. Many instrumental students may have singing voice problems which have gone uncorrected. Instrumental teachers must also be voice teachers and know how to work with children's voice problems. It is beyond the scope of this book to elaborate upon techniques for dealing with singing voice problems, but the reader is urged to consult books by Robert Nye and Edwin Gordon for assistance. [4]

Evidence suggests that without a developed sense of tonality, it is difficult to sing in tune. Further, most instrumentalists play consistently in tune if they sing in tune. Thomas Harris's evidence supports this assumption; he found that vocalization improved instrumental intonation of junior and senior high school instrumentalists. [5] An instrument may be used as a means to express tonality, but a performer must audiate what is to be played and later what is seen in notation in order to play in tune. Robert McGarry reported significant effects of vocalization with below average instrumental achievers. [6] Charles Elliott concluded that daily vocal training is significant in development of a sense of pitch in beginning band classes, and William Schlacks reported that high school band students improved pitch accuracy after training in singing and playing intervals. [7]

Children should also have opportunities for repeated listening to recorded songs with melodies in various modes and with appealing lyrics. It is especially helpful to have recorded examples of materials to be performed. Shinichi Suzuki gives much importance to aural training of stringed instrument players through use of recorded models of tonal music. [8] His purposes are twofold—to develop familiarity with music to be played and to establish a model of tone quality. A third result is aural reinforcement of tonal understandings. Sperti included recorded materials in an adaptation of Suzuki's techniques for teaching beginning clarinetists. [9] Achievement of clarinet students with access to recorded materials was superior to those without recorded models.

Listening and singing constitute the aural/oral foundation upon which a sense of tonality is established. Songs which students already know through singing are the most effective musical material for beginning instrumentalists. This allows an instrument to become an extension of the voice. An instrument becomes a means for musical self-expression rather than a machine to manipulate.

Tunes to be performed on instruments should include lyrics, which facilitates singing and expressiveness. Words also help draw attention to appropriate phrasing and act as reference points for explanations and directions.

Beginning instrumental instruction should regularly include singing tunes before they are played. Students should then be encouraged to play familiar simple tunes "by ear" at many different pitch levels. Fingerings and range expansion can be accomplished without additional material; a musical reason will exist for learning new fingerings. Sound should be emphasized before symbols; that is, students should regularly perform by ear without notation, especially during beginning stages.

Instrumental music programs should have direct connections with elementary general music content—not an original idea but certainly one not evident in most school music programs. Singing in general music classes can be an important basis for instrumental programs. All children should first develop their singing voices for expressing themselves musically. These songs can be arranged and adapted to provide a known repertoire of aural/oral models for instrumental performance.

Recall the experience of using your instrument to sightread a selection which you had heard before but had not seen previously in notation. Usually, the sightreading goes quite well because the sounds produced on the instrument can be compared with the internalized model. On the other hand, when asked to sightread completely unfamiliar music, the difficulty of the task increases dramatically depending upon how much musical meaning the performer gives to the notation. Beginning instrumentalists should not be asked to read totally unfamiliar music without first developing their musical readiness to read notation meaningfully. Otherwise, students become button-pushers to whom notation only indicates what fingers to put down.

Initial Tonal Content

It is generally believed that a sense of tonality is initially developed through an aural affinity for a tonal center or final resting tone. This tone is also known as the key-tone or tonic and is defined as the first scale-tone of a given mode. Underlying harmonic structures also provide aural cues to tonality recognition.

Drawing attention to the final resting tone of many songs sung or played is an important initial activity. Students should be trained to recognize aurally where the resting tone occurs in tunes of various modes. Techniques might include: 1) requesting students to sing and/or play the resting tone to an incomplete phrase or tune, 2) listening to recordings or to the performance of other students or the teacher and recognizing what pitch is the resting tone and indicating when it occurs, 3) having one or two students play only when the resting tone occurs while others sing the tune, and 4) counting how many times the resting tone occurs at phrase endings while hearing or playing a song.

Tonic arpeggios that are sung and/or played prior to or following the performance of songs are helpful for establishment of a sense of mode. In the following examples and in Figure 3.2, the capital letters indicate movable *do* syllables. The lines above or below the syllable letters indicate the pitch direction from the previous syllable. Singing or playing D $\overline{\text{M}}$ $\overline{\text{S}}$ $\underline{\text{M}}$ $\underline{\text{D}}$ or extending to D $\overline{\text{M}}$ $\overline{\text{S}}$ $\underline{\text{M}}$ $\underline{\text{D}}$ T $\overline{\text{D}}$ or D $\overline{\text{R}}$ $\overline{\text{M}}$ $\overline{\text{F}}$ $\overline{\text{S}}$ $\underline{\text{L}}$ $\underline{\text{S}}$ $\underline{\text{M}}$ $\underline{\text{D}}$ $\underline{\text{T}}$ $\overline{\text{D}}$ provides a "home base" for major mode songs. Use L $\overline{\text{D}}$ $\overline{\text{M}}$ $\underline{\text{D}}$ $\underline{\text{L}}$ or L $\overline{\text{D}}$ $\overline{\text{M}}$ $\underline{\text{D}}$ L Si $\overline{\text{L}}$ or L $\overline{\text{T}}$ $\overline{\text{D}}$ $\overline{\text{R}}$ $\overline{\text{M}}$ $\overline{\text{F}}$ $\underline{\text{M}}$ $\underline{\text{D}}$ L Si $\overline{\text{L}}$ with harmonic minor. For those unfamiliar with correct syllable pronunciation, they are phonetically pronounced: *do* = doe, *re* = ray, *mi* = mee, *fa* = fah, *sol* = so, *la* = lah, *ti* = tee.

Figure 3.2 includes tonic arpeggios for six different modes. In each case, the longest arpeggio includes all the characteristic sounds of the particular mode. Students should first be taught to sing the arpeggios by rote and then to play them without notation at as many pitch levels as their range allows. A useful lesson activity is to ask students upon hearing, singing, or playing a major or minor song, "Is it a D M̄ S̄ or a L D̄ M̄ (sing the syllables) song?" and, "Which sounds correct?"

Major   D M̄ S̄ M̲ D̲

                    D M̄ S̄ M̲ D̲ T̲ D̄

                    D R̄ M̄ F̄ S̄ L̄ S̲ M̲ D̲ T̲ D̄

Dorian   R F̄ L̄ F̲ R̲

                    R F̄ L̄ F̲ R̲ D̲ R̄

                    R M̄ F̄ S̄ L̄ T̄ L̲ F̲ R̲ D̲ R̄

Phrygian   M S̄ T̄ S̲ M̲

                    M S̄ T̄ S̲ M̲ R̲ M̄

                    M F̄ S̄ L̄ T̄ D̄ T̲ S̲ M̲ R̲ M̄

Lydian   F L̄ D̄ L̲ F̲

                    F L̄ D̄ L̲ F̲ M̲ F̄

                    F S̄ L̄ T̄ D̄ R̄ D̲ L̲ F̲ M̲ F̄

Mixolydian   S T̄ R̄ T̲ S̲

                    S T̄ R̄ T̲ S̲ F̲ S̄

                    S L̄ T̄ D̄ R̄ M̄ R̲ T̲ S̲ F̲ S̄

Minor   L D̄ M̄ D̲ L̲

                    L D̄ M̄ D̲ L̲ Si̲ L̄

                    L T̄ D̄ R̄ M̄ F̄ M̲ D̲ L̲ Si̲ L̄

Fig. 3.2. Tonic arpeggios for six modes.

Both major and minor mode songs should be used regularly in instrumental instruction so comparisons may be made between the sound of the two modes. After a considerable repertoire of major and minor songs can be performed, introduce songs in dorian and mixolydian. Later on, include songs in phrygian and lydian modes. Songs in modes other than major and minor may be located in folk music from many European countries and in American Indian music and used as supplementary material. Unfortunately, most instrumental materials include far too many major mode songs in proportion to those in minor, and few songs in other modes are included.

Switching Modes

An especially useful technique is to sing or play the same song in two or more modes; for example, the student might perform "Are You Sleeping" in major, then in minor. Be aware of characteristic pitches of the new mode in song melodies when determining what songs may be switched. For example, a natural minor melody without the sixth degree of the minor scale cannot be changed to dorian; a major melody without the seventh degree of the major scale does not change to mixolydian.

Students can often be led into changing the mode of a song without verbal preparation. While the teacher provides a chordal accompaniment, students may sing silently through a song, then sing aloud with the accompaniment. Figure 3.3 includes three primary chords for accompanying in each mode. Note that only major and minor have all three chords in common. When melodies are changed from major or minor to one of the other modes, chordal accompaniments must be changed also for the new mode.

A teaching technique for changing a song that was first learned in major to minor is to preface the song with a minor arpeggio or i-V_7-i chordal progression and begin singing the song. Avoid verbal explanations and notational or theoretical information at this point. After singing through the song in the new mode, give students an appropriate starting pitch and any new fingerings necessary to perform the song on their instruments.

Fig. 3.3.   Key of D chord arpeggios for six modes.

Building a Tonal Pattern Vocabulary

A vocabulary of tonal patterns should be taught with aural resting tone recognition and association of tunes with major and minor tonic arpeggios. Tonal patterns are groups of two to five pitches exclusive of repeated tones. Tonal patterns are related to and derived from underlying harmonic function. Tonal patterns should be sung or played in a steady, moderate tempo without other rhythmic interaction. The determination of tonal pattern parameters within a melody is somewhat arbitrary. Common sense with attention to pitch direction, phrasing, and harmonic function provides workable criteria. The following song text excerpt has the tonal patterns indicated by tonal syllables underneath the words. Pattern length is indicated by slashes (/).

Hot   cross   buns, / hot   cross   buns,
M   R̲   D̲   M   R̲   D̲

One   a-penny,   two   a-penny, / hot   cross   buns, /
D   R̄   M   R   D̲

Notice that in this particular song, two- or three-tone patterns are arbitrarily chosen to fit with the phrase structure. Melodic repetitions of pitches are ignored within each pattern. It is not necessary to teach every tonal pattern in more complex melodies before or after singing and playing the tune. "Hot Cross Buns" is a particularly useful song because of its limited range and pattern content.

Carol MacKnight investigated the effect of tonal pattern training upon achievement of beginning instrumentalists. She concluded that tonal pattern training produces a higher average level of music achievement than does note identification training.[10] Extensive research on development of a tonal pattern taxonomy was done by Edwin Gordon.[11] His research provides information concerning the perceptual difficulty and implied harmonic function of tonal patterns. Music teaching and learning may be greatly enhanced when tonal pattern training is based upon an effective sequence of pattern content.

Patterns are first introduced to students through echo-singing with a neutral syllable such as "loo." The first two to five tone patterns to be taught should be taken from the tonic chord (e.g., D M̄ S̄, D M̄ D̲ in major). Diatonic patterns outlined by chord tones may also be used (e.g., D R̄ M̄, D M̄ F̄ S̄ in major). Students may also echo-play patterns when given correct fingerings.

Using Movable Do

Of the various popular techniques including note names, fixed *do*, and numbers, the movable *do* system is the most efficient means of attaching tonal meaning to patterns of pitches for the purpose of developing a tonal pattern vocabulary and a sense of tonality. In the movable *do* system, syllables are assigned to modes as follows with the first syllable being the resting tone:

Major	*DO re mi fa sol la ti do*
Dorian	*RE mi fa sol la ti do re*
Phrygian	*MI fa sol la ti do re mi*
Lydian	*FA sol la ti do re mi fa*
Mixolydian	*SOL la ti do re mi fa sol*
Minor	*LA ti do re mi fa si la*

Notice in minor mode, *si* is used to provide the harmonic form commonly used in song literature. An advantage of the movable *do* system is that by using a different syllable for the resting tone of each mode, the resulting sequence of whole and half steps is automatically correct for each mode without chromatic alteration of syllables. Intervallic distances between syllables remain constant regardless of mode.

Another advantage of movable *do* syllables is the availability of a systematic and unique monosyllabic set of syllables for chromatic and accidental pitches. Singing only one syllable per tone eliminates any possible rhythmic implication. Raising pitches by half-steps is accomplished by:

do(di) re(ri) mi fa(fi) sol(si) la(li) ti do

Lowering pitches by half-steps occurs as follows:

do ti(te) la(le) sol(se) fa mi(me) re(ra) do

Chromatic syllables are not used for raised *mi* and *ti* or for lowered *fa* and *do* because of the half-step interval between *mi* and *fa* and between *ti* and *do*. They are also unnecessary because beginning song literature rarely includes those chromatic alterations.

Various forms of movable *do* techniques have been found in music teaching in this country since the time of Lowell Mason in the mid-1800s. When used, it has been more widespread in classroom general music than instrumental music teaching. Peter Dykema and

Hannah Cundiff typify much of the practice of movable *do* use in this country through the mid-1900s in their observation that:

> Properly used, scale syllable names: (1) Furnish a correct and helpful method of establishing early in the learner's consciousness, command of the intervals, both step-wise and in leaps, of the major scale, and eventually of all scales. (2) Make music reading in any key equally feasible, because the relative tone relations of scale tones and their names are uniform in all keys. When the correct location of the key or central tone (*do*) is established from the key signature, all other tones naturally fall into the familiar pattern used in every key. (3) Introduce chromatic tones with simple special names which are logically related to the names and musical qualities of the major scale tones. (4) Clarify concepts of transposition and modulation by introducing the transitional tones gradually in easily performed musical material. (5) Form the simplest method now available for enabling the grade teacher to teach and supervise music reading, as has been widely demonstrated by its successful use in schools where there was no other musical equipment than pitch-pipe and music books. (6) Correlate with writing down music heard or originated, and with playing by ear. Many instrumental teachers use them as a means of helping their pupil transpose simple compositions into a variety of keys.[12]

Initial use of tonal syllables should be with the sound and not the notation of two to five tone patterns. The tonal syllables become, in effect, the "words" for sound pattern relationships which appear again and again in melodies at various pitch levels.

Students should not be expected to sing through entire melodies using tonal syllables in melodic rhythm. Initially, tonal syllables should be reserved for learning new patterns and for reinforcing previously learned patterns. Advanced students with a developed vocabulary of tonal patterns may wish to sing syllables melodically throughout entire familiar tunes, but this is not an initial learning activity nor an end in itself.

Echo-singing and echo-playing are essential techniques for building a vocabulary of tonal patterns without notation. The verbal association process is accomplished with the movable *do* syllables. Syllables should be first echo-sung for the patterns without notation. Patterns may then be performed instrumentally at different pitch levels. Introducing the tonic major arpeggio pattern without notation would proceed as follows:

Teacher	Student
1. sings pitches with "lu, lu, lu"	echo-sings
2. sings/plays pitches	echo-plays
3. sings pitches with "D M̄ S̄"	echo-sings
4. sings pitches with "lu, lu, lu"	sings D M̄ S̄
5. sings "D M̄ S̄"	plays pitches
6. gives new fingerings if necessary, asks for D M̄ S̄ with new pitches	plays D M̄ S̄ with new pitches

Tonal Pattern Content

Examples of tonal patterns are displayed in Figure 3.4. The patterns shown are for major and minor modes. The basic patterns consist of pitches from the tonic, dominant seventh, and sub-dominant chords. Patterns from the dominant seventh and sub-dominant chords should be taught after a number of tonic chord patterns are learned. When working with other than tonic chord patterns, be certain to establish the tonality by first echoing tonic arpeggios.

It is often helpful (especially for woodwinds, strings, and keyboards) to use tonal patterns which include appropriate passing tones within the given key. Moving diatonically is an aid in development of smooth fingering technique. Playing in tune and awareness of harmonic function is enhanced when diatonic patterns begin and end with chord tones. Typical beginning patterns in major include: D R̄ M̄, M R̲ D̲, D R̄ M̄ F̄ S̄, S F̲ M̲ R̲ D̲, S L̲ T̄ D̄, and in minor, L T̄ D̄, D T̲ L̲, L T̄ D̄ R̄ M̄, M R̲ D̲ T̲ L̲, M F̄ S̄ L̄.

Tonal patterns based upon supertonic, submediant, and mediant chords may be introduced after basic patterns are learned. Patterns with accidentals and chromatics may also be included as students become more proficient.

More Tonal Pattern Teaching Techniques

As soon as students can play a few patterns, they should be encouraged to make up their own tunes using the patterns. This may be accomplished through singing or playing a chained-together series of familiar patterns with simple articulations and rhythms.

Pitch letter names should be associated with fingerings and used as verbal reference points when playing tonal patterns. Beginning instrumentalists should not be required to learn the names of staff lines and spaces until they have worked aurally with tonal syllables

Fig. 3.4   Selected beginning tonal patterns for major modes.

Fig. 3.4 (Continued). Selected beginning tonal patterns for minor modes.

and patterns. Names of written notes are learned functionally as familiar tonal patterns are associated with symbols. Letter names are also used to label instrument fingerings.

Tonal syllables must not be exclusively associated with fingerings or letter names whenever new patterns are introduced. It is important to learn any given tonal pattern at more than one pitch level concurrently so that fingerings are not always associated with particular tonal syllables. Transposition becomes an easy process when a tonal pattern vocabulary is practiced at many pitch levels. Beginning songs should also be regularly performed at more than one starting pitch, and new fingerings should be given as needed.

An Arpeggio Worksheet is shown in Figure 3.5. Columns of syllables should be read as arpeggios from bottom to top to bottom—D $\overline{M}$ $\overline{S}$ $\underline{M}$ $\underline{D}$, D $\overline{F}$ $\overline{L}$ $\underline{F}$ $\underline{D}$, etc. Different students in a class may simultaneously sing or play the horizontal lines—S $\overline{L}$ $\underline{S}$ S S, M $\overline{F}$ $\underline{M}$ $\overline{F}$ $\underline{M}$, D D D $\underline{T}$ $\overline{D}$ to sound the chord progression. Each chord of simultaneously sounded columns of syllables may be repeated before moving to the next one. Holding up one, four, or five fingers as a visual cue for a chord permits changing the order of chords during performance. The number of repetitions of each chord may be predetermined or indicated during performance. Simple tunes may be chordally accompanied by a minimum of three class members while the teacher or another student indicates appropriate chord changes. Individuals may improvise melodic patterns on underlying chord progressions provided by the class. The arpeggios and chord accompaniments in both major and minor should be emphasized and eventually learned in all keys.

In instrumental training, tonal patterns should generally relate directly to tunes which are sung and played. After learning to sing and play a tune, tonal patterns may be extracted and practiced alone. It is not necessary to deal with all possible patterns in a melody. Students might be asked to discover the frequency of a given pattern within a song or to recall other familiar songs which incorporate the same pattern. Other activities should include: 1) organizing patterns in the order in which they occur in a particular song; 2) rearranging the tonal patterns of a familiar song to create a different song; and 3) altering patterns within a song to create melodic variation. This should first be done aurally with syllables and later, with notation.

Consider the following tonal patterns: D $\overline{S}$ $\overline{L}$ $\underline{S}$, F $\underline{M}$ $\underline{R}$ $\underline{D}$, S $\underline{F}$ $\underline{M}$ $\underline{R}$. Students could echo-sing and play the patterns and then be asked if any songs are known which include these patterns. "Twinkle, Twinkle, Little Star" could then be sung and/or played. The three patterns may be recognized as constituting the melody of the song.

ARPEGGIO WORKSHEET

S	L	S	S	S	I can play this with do as:
M	F	M	F	M	————
			(R)		————
D	D	D	T D	D	————
					————
					————
I	IV	I	V7	I	————

M	F	M	M	M	I can play this with la as:
D	R	D	R	D	————
			(T)		————
L	L	L	Si L	L	————
					————
					————
i	iv	i	V7	i	————

Fig. 3.5.   An arpeggio worksheet.

Dialogue techniques are especially useful for developing tonal pattern vocabularies. Variations include: 1) the student performs the A sections of a simple tonal pattern rondo while the teacher intersperses contrasting patterns; 2) the teacher performs the A sections of a simple tonal pattern rondo while individual students intersperse contrasting patterns; 3) students each perform a chain of different patterns without teacher interaction. The patterns may be sung with syllables or played with instruments. Individual differences may be met within class groupings. See Appendix A for more applications of dialogue techniques.

Tonal patterns may also be used as ostinatos for simple tunes. Students may be encouraged to discover which patterns function as ostinatos with specific tunes. Small sections of rounds may be used as tonal ostinatos to accompany the melody of the round.

The development of a sense of tonality and a tonal pattern vocabulary is enhanced by the use of harmonic accompaniments. Consider using guitar, autoharp, or piano on a regular basis for providing harmonic accompaniments to instrumental lesson material. A cadential chord progression used as an introduction to melodies can establish the mode and tonality for the performers. The tonal function of any given pitch in a melody is immediately more obvious if harmonic reinforcement is available. Playing in tune becomes generally easier and more accurate with chordal accompaniment.

Reading Tonal Notation

Most traditional approaches to instrumental training begin with the association of fingerings and notation. This visual process is often nonmusical, boring, difficult, and musically unproductive for students. The readiness for reading music notation is demonstrated when simple tunes can be sung and played and when tonal patterns can be performed with syllables and instruments. Fingering patterns should first be associated aurally with tonal patterns. Songs and tonal patterns that have been performed without notation should be the first examples to be seen with notation. The intention is to associate musical sounds with notation, not to attempt to extract musical sounds from notation.

The readiness sequence for reading tonal symbols begins with rote singing and playing of simple tunes and tonal patterns as described in earlier sections of this chapter. A critical interim step is the association of movable *do* syllables with the functional sound of tonal patterns. Students are ready to read the patterns when they can associate and sing the correct syllables with sounded patterns. It is possible at this point to attach musical meaning to notation. The symbols are then representative of the tonal pattern vocabulary and are visual cues for specific fingerings, a process analogous to learning to speak before learning to read. The sequence for moving from syllable association sounds to notation for a given familiar pattern could be as follows:

Teacher	Student
Sings M R D	Echo-sings M R D
Plays M R D	Echo-plays M R D
Sings lu(M), lu(R), lu(D)	Echo-sings M R D
Shows notation for M R D	Sings M R D, plays M R D
New notation for M R D	Sings M R D, plays M R D

The pattern should be shown in a new key as soon as students can consistently read it in the familiar key. Students should also copy notation of familiar patterns as a prerequisite to tonal dictation and composition.

It is not necessary to precede reading music notation with reading other less exact representations of pitches or melodic direction. This would be analogous to insisting that children should learn to read a pre-alphabet set of symbols before learning the real alphabet symbols. When first reading music, special attention should be drawn to "on the line," meaning the line runs through the note head, and "in the space," meaning the note head is between lines, not on the line. Reading music notation is appropriate after tonal readiness has been acquired.

One of the most effective and practical techniques for teaching music reading is the use of flash cards of familiar tonal patterns. Gradually introduce the familiar patterns in various keys in major and minor on flash cards. Choice of keys should depend upon appropriate instrument ranges. Each card should include a correct key signature. Cards should be organized by chord function (tonic, dominant-seventh, sub-dominant, and so on for major and minor) of patterns within keys.

Notes should be called by letter names as they are associated with lines and spaces in pattern configurations on the flash cards. Fingerings which have been called by note names are then easily associated with staff notation.

Activities with flash cards may include: singing correct syllables and playing the patterns on the cards; recognizing patterns in notated songs which match the flash card patterns; creating new tunes by organizing various series of cards; recognizing which cards are being performed by other students; and copying notation from cards. These activities may take place in class or individual lessons or in large rehearsal groups. Brief but regular practice with flash cards of patterns which appear in familiar tunes is an important means toward development of vocabulary and a sense of tonality.

Instrumentalists need to know how to interpret key signatures after music reading begins. Key signatures can give musical information if thought of as *do* signatures, i.e., symbols which visually locate the line or space for *do*. *Do* is located with sharp key signatures by beginning with the sharp sign farthest right as number one and counting down lines and spaces to seven. In flat key signatures, begin with the flat sign farthest right as number one and count down lines and spaces to four (or the next to the last flat in key signatures with more than one flat). Counting down to *do* rather than up visually places the note for *do* on the staff and in the correct range for beginners. The location of the tone for any tonal syllable is easily interpreted after *do* is located. Students should become aware of some of the visual relationships of pitches on the staff by observing when *do* is on a line, *mi* and *sol* are on the next lines above; when *do* is on a space, *mi* and *sol* are on the next spaces above; etc.

The letter name of the tonic resting tone becomes the key name, and the tonal syllable for the tonic resting tone indicates the mode name. For example, resting tone is A_b and *re* = A_b dorian (6 flats); resting tone is B and *la* = B minor (2 sharps); resting tone is B and sol = B mixolydian (4 sharps). See Figure 3.1 for comparisons. The order of sharps and flats in a key signature should be memorized. A mnemonic device useful for the order of sharps is "Fat Cats Get Drowsy After Eating Birds." The order of flats may be learned as the reverse of the sharps.

Reading unfamiliar music (sightreading) is basically recognizing familiar patterns in new settings. Music for sightreading is of an appropriate difficulty level when the majority of patterns are familiar. This allows success and motivation for most students. After students begin to read songs that they can already sing and play, opportunities for reading unfamiliar songs of the same difficulty level must be provided on a regular basis. Generalizing from the known to the unknown is facilitated through this practice. A helpful ongoing lesson assignment is for students to choose and prepare for performance a song of their choice from a song collection book. The interaction of rhythm and tonal patterns with sightreading is discussed further in chapters 4 and 5.

It is essential that as students begin to read music, they also write music. Learning to read and write concurrently develops understanding of symbols for musical sounds more fully and encourages manipulation of the symbols through arranging and composition. The mechanics of writing music may be acquired by careful copying of tonal flash cards and simple familiar tunes. Tunes learned in one key should be written and performed in new keys. Students can compose new endings or variations of tunes, or compose settings for simple poems. Regular written assignments are appropriate when music reading begins. Dictation exercises of patterns and tunes are appropriate as students gain writing facility.

When beginning notation reading, movable *do* syllables are the verbal associations with familiar tonal patterns which are now represented by symbols. The syllables should not be used to sing through entire melodies but should be restricted for tonal pattern identification. Composite synthesis (CS) activities may include recognizing familiar patterns with syllable labels in notation. The intent is for students to develop audiation facility (to hear what they see) without overtly thinking of each individual note or tonal syllable. This occurs in language reading when one no longer reads individual letters or words, but instead, reads phrases as expressions of meaning.

Other Modes

It was mentioned earlier in this chapter that songs in modes other than major and minor should also be taught and learned as a part of instrumental music. Singing and playing songs in several different modes increases tonal vocabularies and aids a sense of tonality. When students are reading tunes in major and minor, it is appropriate to begin singing songs and learning patterns in other modes. Dorian, a minor-related mode, and mixolydian, a major-related mode, should be introduced first. After dorian and mixolydian songs are established, introduce material in phrygian and lydian. The sequence for introducing songs and tonal patterns in other modes is the same as for major and minor. Songs should be sung and played; tonic arpeggios with correct syllables should be learned (see Figure 3.2); and tonal patterns relating to chords (see Figure 3.3) should be taught. Notation should be gradually introduced for familiar songs and patterns.

It is necessary and desirable to change major or minor melodies into other modes; how to do so melodically without using notation was described earlier in this chapter. When students have aural readiness for modes and are reading notation accurately, it is possible to change modes of notated melodies by altering key signatures. The melody is performed in a new mode by reading the same notes with a different key signature. Minor songs may be changed to dorian by adding a sharp to or removing a flat from the minor key signature. Minor songs may be changed to phrygian by adding a flat or removing a sharp. Major songs change to mixolydian by adding a flat or removing a sharp and to lydian by adding a sharp or removing a flat. These changes are only possible melodically because underlying chordal accompaniments are different when switching major or minor songs to other modes. Accompaniments for the changed songs would need to be altered with some different chords and cadences (see Figure 3.3).

Tonal Music Theory

Many music teachers insist on teaching music theory when children begin reading music. It is unnecessary and usually undesirable to teach music theory to beginning music readers because it does not help them function musically. If music theory is introduced, it should occur only after students are accomplished music readers with a functional tonal (and rhythm) vocabulary. Knowledge of grammar and parts of speech does not precede speaking, reading, and writing of a language; neither can theoretical knowledge substitute for musical skills. Typical tonal music theory information that may be taught when appropriate includes intervals and why the location of two half-steps (always represented with *mi-fa* and *ti-do*) within a scale determines the mode.

Choosing Materials

The basic materials for beginning instrumentalists are songs that can be sung and played in appropriate ranges. Folk music and songs from general music classes are particularly useful. A list of songs categorized by range appears in Appendix B. These songs may be sung and played without notation, transposed and later read at different pitch levels, performed with switched modes, and used as bases for creative and improvisational activities to develop a sense of tonality and a tonal pattern vocabulary.

Materials should be chosen to teach tonal content objectives. It is helpful for the teacher to develop source files of familiar tunes which work well to teach specific tonal content. The primary goal is to teach the sequence of tonal content through song literature, not just to teach a collection of songs.

Tonal Objectives

The following list of tonal objectives for instrumentalists incorporates the tonal content with the Gordon learning sequence levels (indicated in parentheses). It is intended as an organizational guide for tonal instruction with beginning instrumentalists regardless of age level. Note that beginning with objective number 6 the content is specific for major and minor tonic function tonal patterns. Similar sequences of objectives 6 through 17 are overlapped simultaneously as indicated. The pacing of the overlapping content must be determined by the teacher after assessment of student achievement. Individual student needs should always be taken into consideration. Recognize also that other similar lists could be constructed with variations in content.

The student will be able to:

1.   sing/play familiar major and minor songs without notation (A/O).

2.   sing/play major and minor tonic arpeggios with syllables but without notation (VA).

3.   recognize aurally major and minor resting tones (A/O).

4.   label familiar songs as in major or minor mode after hearing or performing without notation (VA).

5.   label unfamiliar songs as in major or minor mode after hearing without notation (G).

6.   echo-sing/play major and minor tonic function tonal patterns without syllables or notation (A/O).

7.   echo-sing major and minor tonic function tonal patterns with tonal syllables and without notation (VA).

8.   sing major and minor tonic function tonal patterns with tonal syllables after hearing patterns performed without notation (VA).

9.   recognize aurally major and minor tonic function tonal pat-

terns in familiar songs without notation (PS). (At this point, overlap objectives by simultaneously beginning a content sequence at number 6 with major and minor dominant-seventh function tonal patterns.)

10. recognize aurally major and minor tonic function tonal patterns in unfamiliar songs without notation (G).

11. sing with syllables and play self-created combinations of familiar major and minor tonic function tonal patterns without notation (C/I). (At this point, overlap objectives by simultaneously beginning a content sequence at number 6 with major and minor subdominant function tonal patterns.)

12. recognize familiar major and minor tonic function tonal patterns in notation (SA).

13. sing with syllables, write, and play notated major and minor tonic function tonal patterns (SA). (At this point, overlap objectives by simultaneously beginning a content sequence at number 6 with supertonic, submediant, mediant function and chromatic tonal patterns.)

14. recognize, sing/play familiar major and minor tonic function tonal patterns within notation of familiar songs (CS).

15. recognize, sing/play familiar major and minor tonic function tonal patterns within notation of unfamiliar songs (G).

16. improvise, compose, and perform combinations of familiar written major and minor tonic function tonal patterns (C/I).

17. understand the theoretical basis for harmonic function of major and minor tonic function tonal patterns (TU).

Tonal patterns in dorian, mixolydian, phrygian, and lydian modes may be introduced and taught in the preceding sequence of objectives by making appropriate content changes (see Figure 3.3 for chords). Additional lists of pattern objectives would also require overlapping. It is not desirable or necessary to complete the entire list for one segment of content before beginning a new segment.

The task of teaching a sense of tonality is not formidable, and teachers should be encouraged to learn and practice through their teaching. A lack of experience and practice with teaching tonal patterns and modes on the part of teachers should not become a limitation placed upon instrumental students.

Review Questions

1. What is a sense of tonality?
2. What tonal readiness activity is essential to beginning instrumentalists?
3. Upon what is singing and playing in tune dependent?
4. Why should tunes for beginning instrumentalists include the words?
5. What consitutes the aural/oral level for a sense of tonality?
6. Why should songs in modes other than major be taught?
7. What is a tonal pattern?
8. Why should beginning instrumentalists develop a tonal pattern vocabulary?
9. How are tonal patterns taught with Verbal Association?
10. When and how should beginning instrumentalists be introduced to music notation?
11. What is the rationale for interpreting key signatures and naming keys?
12. What is the purpose of writing music notation and taking dictation?
13. Considering the tonal pattern D $\overline{\text{M}}$ $\overline{\text{S}}$, what would be an appropriate teaching technique at each level of the Gordon Learning Sequence for beginning instrumentalists?
14. What is the sequence of tonal content discussed in this chapter?

4

TEACHING RHYTHMIC FEELING

TRADITIONAL instrumental teaching places great emphasis upon rhythmic accuracy as indicated by symbols for proportional note values. Rhythm errors are often the first detected by instructors of lessons and rehearsals. Correction of rhythm errors usually involves reference to the mathematics of note durations rather than the underlying rhythmic feeling and flow. As a result, performances often sound mechanical and nonmusical.

Defining Rhythmic Feeling

Musicians and others have created many definitions of rhythm that attempt to be precise and all-encompassing. Most traditional explanations emphasize the duration of musical sounds and then include music notation as examples of proportional note values. Instead of musical sounds taught with rhythmic feeling, the visual and mathematical aspects of rhythm notation become the emphasis of instruction. Many problems result because the symbols used to represent rhythms are often inadequate to express intent accurately. Rhythm notation becomes most meaningful when rhythmic understandings are represented by the symbols and not derived from the symbols.

The problems of teaching rhythmic feeling are not a recent phenomenon. James Mursell and Mabelle Glenn note that they

> would regard counting, foot tapping, and the minute study of temporal durations as open to question. As to counting and foot tapping, these are poor ways of generating a sense of rhythm. Instrumental in-

structors who build wholly upon them ignore the previous rhythmic experience set up in the vocal program. (Of course in some vocal work, no sense of rhythm is built up, and then there is nothing to transfer.) What is wanted is not a sense of one-two-three-four, etc., etc., but a sense of the swing of the music . . . . We may work so hard for mathematically accurate time values, that the pupil thinks of nothing else, and completely loses hold of the rhythmic swing. [1]

Rhythmic flow is the durational organizer of musical sounds. Rhythmic feeling results when the listener or performer responds by perceiving and organizing musical sounds in meaningful patterns without the aid of notation.

Students may be trained to have a sense of rhythmic feeling as well as a sense of tonality. It is possible for almost everyone to improve memory and recognition of rhythms. Rhythms become familiar in music through repeated listening, physical response, and development of a pattern vocabulary. Emile-Jacques Dalcroze stated, "By means of movements of the whole body, we may equip ourselves to realize and perceive rhythms." [2] Rhythmic understanding is aided by anticipation and expectation while listening and performing.

Nearly all Western music has an underlying rhythmic organizer commonly referred to as the beat or pulse. The terms "beat" and "pulse" often have different connotations among musicians and nonmusicians and have limited precision of meaning when referring to rhythmic feeling. Rhythm is more than a usually obvious "beat." It is helpful to describe and learn rhythmic feeling by working with its various components. To describe the rhythm of a piece of music accurately requires more meaningful terminology with regard to rhythmic feeling. Terminology must also be understandable and usable by very young children as well as adults. The system of terms for describing rhythmic feeling used throughout this chapter first appeared in Edwin Gordon's *The Psychology of Music Teaching*, [3] in which Gordon defines rhythm as comprising tempo beats, meter beats, and melodic rhythm.

Tempo beat refers to the recurring underlying feeling in music which acts as the primary rhythmic organizer. Most metronome markings in music refer to the speed or tempo of this beat. Each underlying tempo beat in the tune of the following song text excerpts is indicated by an x.

Yan-kee	Doo-dle	went	to	town,
x	x	x		x

Rid-ing	on	a	po-	ny
x	x		x	x

```
Where,   oh   where   has my   lit-tle   dog   gone?
x              x              x          x
Where,   oh   where   can   he   be - - - - - - - - -?
x              x              x          x
```

Meter beats occur when two or three even subdivisions are superimposed upon tempo beats. Perception of underlying meter beat feeling as tempo beat subdivisions enables a listener to define the rhythmic feeling of music as moving in duple or triple meter. (An exception to this will be discussed later.) As with tempo beats, accurate recognition and feeling for meter is essential for meaningful music listening and performance. The underlying meter beats are indicated with - - or - - - and an x indicates tempo beats in the following song text examples:

```
Jin-gle   bells,   jin-gle   bells,
-  -       -  -     -  -  -     -  -
x         x        x         x

jin-gle   all   the   way
-  -       -     -     -  -  -  -
x         x         x   x

Here   we   go   round   the   mul-ber-ry   bush,   the
-        -     -     -    -    -   -    -    -    -  -    -
x              x              x              x

mul-ber-ry       bush,   the   mul-ber-ry   bush
-   -   -          -    -    -   -    -    -    -  -    -
x              x              x              x
```

Melodic rhythm patterns are the last component in the definition of rhythmic feeling. Rhythm patterns are the linear building blocks of rhythmic feeling which interact with tones to produce melody (e.g., the rhythm of song texts). Melodic rhythm patterns are superimposed upon underlying tempo beat and meter beat feeling. The rhythmic flow and feeling of a melodic line is dependent upon the underlying tempo beats and meter beats. Rhythm patterns may subdivide, elongate, or coincide with underlying tempo beats and meter beats. Rhythm patterns interact with tonal patterns to create melodies but are learned without tonal implications.

Most melodic rhythm patterns may be arbitrarily defined by whatever occurs within one tempo beat. Exceptions occur with patterns which elongate across tempo beats. Most melodies consist of very few rhythm patterns. For example, melodic rhythm patterns are separated in the following song texts by slashes (/):

Drink to me / on - ly / with thine / eyes, and /
I will / pledge with / mine /

Hang down your / head, Tom / Doo-ley,/
Hang down your / head and / cry /

When a functional rhythm pattern vocabulary is developed, music takes on a meaningful dimension of understanding. A rhythm pattern vocabulary is acquired in the same basic manner that a speaking vocabulary is learned. Sounds are first perceived aurally and then practiced orally as labels (words or syllables) for specific meanings. Written symbols are then taught as representations of the sounds. As the vocabulary grows and becomes a means of expression, the depth of understanding and conceptualization increases.

Rhythm Readiness

A common practice when teaching beginning instrumentalists is to require students to read rhythm notation and "count" accurately while concurrently learning the technical skills of an instrument. This approach frequently ignores the proper readiness necessary to accomplish this complex task. The musical background of typical beginning instrumentalists includes a repertoire of a few familiar songs and some acquaintance with the names of music symbols. This background experience is important but is inadequate rhythm readiness. Most students come to instrumental training with little or no functional rhythm pattern vocabulary. A sense of rhythm is not acquired by memorizing proportional note values; instrumental teachers must provide the appropriate readinesses.

Rhythm readiness begins with kinesthetic response through large muscle movements to music. This may occur informally to some extent through dance and free movement response while listening to music. Dalcroze was one of the first to recognize the connection of large muscle movement to rhythm response and musical development.[4] His efforts to include eurhythmics as a part of musical training have had some influence on general classroom music teaching in this country. The readiness to develop and later read a functional rhythm pattern vocabulary begins with consistent large muscle response to tempo beats. Large muscle movements such as body swaying, rocking, or marching may be readily associated with tempo beat feeling. Accurate meter beat response may then be emphasized as a foundation for a vocabulary of melodic rhythm patterns.

Initial Rhythm Content

If students are to perform music rhythmically with instruments, it is essential that initial content provide appropriate readiness activities and reinforcement. Activities which aid consistent tempo beat response while students are listening to music include: marching, dancing, swaying, rocking as if sitting in a rocking chair, and moving the arms from the shoulders. Foot-tapping is not a large muscle movement and is not appropriate as a beginning activity. Foot-tapping may act as a useful rhythm cue only after feeling for consistent tempo beat speed is firmly established.

Movement activities for meter beat feeling may be included while students demonstrate consistent physical response to tempo beats. In order for a consistent physical response to be associated with duple and triple meter feeling, teach specific movement patterns for each meter. Duple meter feeling is associated with pat-clap movements, and triple meter feeling is associated with pat-clap-clap movements. Pats correspond to the tempo beat feeling, and claps correspond with meter beats. Pat-clap movements should involve the entire arm by moving from the shoulders, the open palms patting on the thighs or clapping together. Meter feeling movements should be evenly spaced. Pat-claps would occur with the following song text excerpts as indicated by the p's and c's under the words:

```
Lon - - don    bridge is      fall - ing     down--,
p        c     p      c        p      c       p      c
fall - ing     down - - - ,    fall - - ing   down - -
p      c       p                p        c     p      c
```

```
Oh  - ,   how love -   ly  is        the  eve  -   ning,
p     c   c    p   c   c   p    c    c    p    c    c
is        the eve -    ning,
p     c   c    p   c   c
```

The teacher should choose music with moderate tempo beat speed that remains constant throughout the melody. It is important that the tempo beat speed allow for comfortable, accurate pat-clap or pat-clap-clap responses. If music moves very slowly, it is difficult to maintain even meter feeling, and if music moves very rapidly, it is difficult to perceive and physically respond to the meter feeling.

When rhythm problems occur in group lessons or rehearsals, it is often helpful to have some students pat tempo beats only, some pat-clap or pat-clap-clap meter beats, and others play or sing the melody. Groups may rotate assignments as they gain proficiency in maintaining the rhythmic flow. Tempo beat movements (pats) and meter beat movements (pat-clap or pat-clap-clap) then become a rhythm accompaniment for melodies by emphasizing the underlying rhythmic feeling. The criterion for determining tempo beat and meter beat feeling is always the sound and feel of the music, never the notation.

Music does not necessarily have to move with evenly spaced tempo beats subdivided into twos and threes. Unusual meter feeling occurs when tempo beats are unevenly spaced and meter beats move in equal durations of twos and threes. Examples are compositions which have a 5 or 7 as the top number of their meter signature. Meter beat movements should again coincide with the groupings of twos and threes which are determined by the tempo beat locations. Unusual meters will be discussed in more detail later in this chapter.

Building a Melodic Rhythm Pattern Vocabulary

Melodic rhythm patterns are small units of the linear movement of melody. The patterns follow the rhythm of the words in songs with texts. Secure tempo beat and meter beat feeling is the foundation upon which accurate melodic rhythm patterns are performed. Most of the time, melodic rhythm patterns may be limited to what occurs within one tempo beat. Rhythm patterns should include more than one tempo beat whenever melodic pitches are held (elongated) across the underlying tempo beat feeling. The following song text examples have the melodic rhythm patterns separated by slashes, the meter beat feeling indicated with p c or p c c, and the tempo beats indicated by x:

```
Koo-ka bur-ra / sits      on the/old      gum / tree/
p        c      p        c       p        c      p        c
x                x                x                x

O  -  ver    the / riv - er    and / through    the / woods      to /
p     c    c    p    c      c    p    c      c    p    c      c
x                    x                x                x
```

Notice that the rhythm patterns may or may not coincide with the tempo beat and meter beat locations. The underlying tempo beat and meter beat feeling remains constant regardless of the rhythm patterns in the melody.

Clapping rhythm patterns is a simple way to associate them with physical movement. Clapping should involve arm and hand movement, not just wrists and hands. Confusion with pat-clap movements for meter beat feeling is avoided by associating rhythm pattern clapping with hand clapping only. Three separate movement associations are then available for rhythm practice with tempo beats (pats), meter beats (pat-clap or pat-clap-clap), and patterns (clapping). Groups of students may be subdivided and assigned the three different movements to be performed simultaneously while others play instruments.

Using Rhythm Syllables

Rhythm syllables are frequently used in traditional instrumental teaching, the most common ones being "1-e-and-a" and "1-and-a." Others include "1-la-li," "1-ta-te-ta," and "ta-a-a-a." There are many inconsistencies in the use and associations of these systems, but the most serious problem is that almost without exception, the systems are taught concurrently with notation as a means of learning proportional note values. Rhythm syllables are traditionally used to teach notation, not rhythmic feeling or aural rhythm patterns. Inefficiency and confusion results from attempting to derive musical meaning *from* notation rather than to bring musical meaning *to* notation.

In order to learn a vocabulary of rhythm patterns efficiently and effectively, a system of verbal association with the sound of patterns is necessary. Using syllables to label rhythm sounds is convenient and practical. A syllable system should be monosyllabic and easy to speak or chant by very young children as well as adults. No syllables should duplicate those used in tonal patterns, and different but related syllables should be used for duple, triple, and unusual meters. Rhythm syllables should not be confused with articulation or tonguing syllables used with wind instruments. Syllables should never be introduced concurrently with notation; they are intended for initial use only with pattern sounds. Syllables should not be chanted melodically throughout entire tunes; again, they are intended for use only with pattern sounds. Clear associations with feeling and sound must be established if rhythm syllables are to have a meaningful purpose.

A rhythm syllable system which meets all of the above stated criteria was adapted by Gordon from a system authored by McHose and Tibbs. [5] Tempo beat locations within patterns are labeled with the numbers 1 or 2 in duple and triple meters. Meter beat locations for duple feeling are given the syllable ne (nay) and for triple feeling, na (nah) ni (nee). All further subdivisions receive the syllable ta (tah). Unusual meter receives different but related syllables with be (bay) for duple feeling and ba (bah) bi (bee) for triple feeling subdivisions of tempo beats. Tempo beats in unusual meters are assigned the syllable du (doo) rather than numbers to avoid confusion when grouped unevenly.

The following examples illustrate how the rhythm syllables superimpose upon the underlying tempo and meter beat feeling:

Duple Meter:

1	ta	ne	ta	2	ta	ne	ta
1		ne		2		ne	
1				2			
p		c		p		c	

Triple Meter:

1	ta	na	ta	ni	ta	2	ta	na	ta	ni	ta
1		na		ni		2		na		ni	
1						2					
p	c		c			p	c		c		

Unusual Meter: (e.g., only for upper number of meter signature as 5)

du	ta	be	ta	du	ta	ba	ta	bi	ta
du		be		du		ba		bi	
du				du					
p		c		p		c		c	

or

du	ta	ba	ta	bi	ta	du	ta	be	ta
du		ba		bi		du		be	
du						du			
p		c		c		p		c	

This rhythm syllable system has received some research interest (Dittemore, DeYarman, and Palmer [6]), and considerable success in field development experiences with music teachers throughout the country.

Rhythm syllables, meter beat feeling, and tempo beat feeling are indicated under the following patterns which are separated by slashes in these song text examples:

```
Koo-ka bur-ra / sits    on the/old    gum / tree /
1    ta ne ta  2      ne ta  1       ne     2
p       c     p     c      p     c     p
x             x            x           x
```

```
O - ver  the / riv - er   and / through  the / woods    to /
1    na   ni   2     na   ni   1          ni   2         ni
p    c    c    p     c    c    p     c    c    p     c    c
x              x               x               x
```

```
Lon - don / bridge is  /  fall - ing / down, /
1     ta    2      ne    1      ne    2
p     c     p      c     p      c     p      c
x           x            x             x
```

```
Here  we  go / round   the / mul - ber ry  /  bush,   the /
1     na  ni   2        ni   1    na  ni    2        ni
p     c   c    p    c   c    p    c   c     p    c    c
x             x              x               x
```

```
We    wish   you   a    mer - ry /  Christ - mas,   we /
ni    1      na    ta   ni    ta   2         na     ni
c     p      c           c          p         c      c
      x                              x
```

Notice that the rhythm syllables fit with the rhythm of the words. Some of the patterns coincide with underlying tempo and meter beat feeling; others further subdivide the meter or tempo beat feeling.

More Rhythm Pattern Teaching Techniques

It becomes obvious that most melodies found in beginning and intermediate instrumental music consist of very few rhythm patterns. Furthermore, these same few rhythm patterns are used again and again and are repeated in different combinations throughout music of the western world. Figure 4.1 contains notation for eleven duple and fifteen triple meter rhythm patterns. The first nine duple patterns and the first four triple patterns account for nearly all beginning song literature found in instrumental method books. By learning to recognize aurally, to associate syllables, to read, and to write a vocabulary of relatively few rhythm patterns, students should be able to perform with rhythmic feeling and accuracy.

After consistent tempo and meter beat feeling is demonstrated, students should begin work aurally with patterns. The first patterns taught should be ones which coincide with the tempo and meter beat feelings in duple and triple (patterns D1, D2, T1 and T2 in Figure 4.1). Patterns should be clapped, chanted, and played. Rhythm patterns should relate to familiar tunes which are sung and played so their recognition and use is continually reinforced.

The sequence of learning rhythm begins with physical response to tempo beat and meter beat feeling in duple and triple. Acquiring a pattern vocabulary begins with echo-clapping of tempo and meter beat patterns without syllables or notation. Echo-clapping and dialogue activities with a few patterns at a time establish familiarity with the sound and feeling of the rhythms. When doing pattern activities, students may realize the underlying tempo beat feeling by rocking slightly forward and back from the hips for duple meter and by swaying slightly from side to side for triple meter. In groups of students, a few may be assigned tempo beat movements, a few meter beat movements, and others clap patterns. Pitches may be given to echo-play rhythm patterns on instruments.

Rhythm syllables should be added when facility for echo-clapping a few patterns is achieved. Association of rhythm syllables to patterns is easily accomplished by echo-chanting and dialogue activities. While maintaining a consistent tempo beat feeling, the teacher chants a pattern and students immediately repeat it in tempo. Chanted syllable responses should always be within the given tempo. The complexity of the task increases when the teacher only claps the patterns and students must answer in rhythm by chanting the correct syllables. Verbal association has taken place when students can consistently demonstrate the correct syllable chanting for clapped patterns, and at that point, they are ready to see the patterns in notation. Additional patterns are introduced through the same process of echo-clapping. Again, patterns should be chosen from familiar songs in duple and triple meter.

Tempo beats are generally perceived and grouped aurally in pairs regardless of the meter feeling. Therefore, the process of echo-chanting beginning patterns is aided by chanting patterns across pairs of tempo beats. By combining patterns over two pairs of tempo beats, a rhythmic phrase is implied. Clapping, chanting, and playing patterns in groups of four tempo beats is a useful practice. Pat-

Fig. 4.1.   Melodic rhythm patterns for duple (D)
and triple (T) meter feelings.

terns may first be repeated for each tempo beat and then later changed on each tempo beat to add complexity. For example:

		Teacher								Student Response					

(Duple patterns)

1		2		1		2		1		2		1		2
1	ne	2	ne	1	ne	2		1	ne	2	ne	1	ne	2
1		2	ne	1	ne	2		1		2	ne	1	ne	2

(Triple patterns)

1		2		1		2		1		2		1		2
1		2	na ni	1	na ni	2		1		2	na ni	1	na ni	2
1	na ni	2		1	na ni	2		1	na ni	2		1	na ni	2
1	na ni	2	na ni	1				1	na ni	2	na ni	1		

More than one repetition may be given each set of patterns. New patterns are readily assimilated when inserted as the second or third tempo beat in the groupings of four. The difficulty level of a set of four patterns increases when a subdivided pattern is used on the fourth tempo beat. For example, the following sets of four patterns each may be echoed:

1	ne	2 ta ne ta 1	ne	2 ta ne ta
1	ne	2	ne	1 ta ne	2 ta ne
1	ne	2	ne ta 1	ne ta 2

1	na	ni	2 ta na ta ni ta 1	na	ni	2
1	na	ni	2 na ta ni ta 1	na ta ni ta 2
1	na	ni	2 ni ta 1	ta ni	2

Figure 4.2 lists the correct syllables for the patterns appearing in Figure 4.1. It is critical for the reader to understand that the rhythm syllables should never be introduced to students in conjunction with notation. It is done here only because of the limitations of the printed word in describing musical sounds. Syllables are only intended for use with the sound of the rhythm patterns. Rhythm syllables should not associate with specific note values. The patterns in Figure 4.1 are only one representation of the sounds. Different symbols are used later to represent the familiar sounds.

As a pattern vocabulary with syllable associations is acquired, and before notation is introduced, it is important to allow opportunities

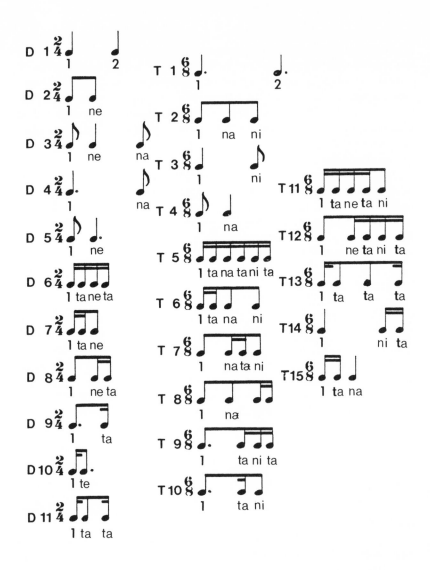

Fig. 4.2. Melodic rhythm patterns with syllables for duple (D)
and triple (T) meter feelings.

for students to utilize their new vocabulary. Activities might include: aurally recognizing where certain patterns occur in familiar and unfamiliar songs, listing familiar songs which begin with or contain a particular pattern or series of patterns, counting how many times a pattern occurs within a song, substituting or rearranging patterns in familiar tunes, stringing familiar patterns together while playing a given pitch, playing strings of patterns as rhythm rounds on given pitches with others, and improvising rhythmic variations on familiar tunes.

Duple and triple songs should be taught concurrently so comparison of meter feeling is possible. Very few triple meter songs are found in beginning instrumental music books. Method books can often be supplemented with triple meter folk songs or popular tunes. A list of triple meter songs appears in Appendix D.

Switching Meters

A valuable technique for teaching a sense of meter is to switch the meter feeling of familiar songs. This may be done with or without notation. The tempo beat feeling must remain in the same location when switching the meter of a song. Meters of songs are readily switched by first establishing the correct physical movement for the new meter. For example, audiate the first phrase of "Yankee Doodle" with the following duple syllables and pat-claps:

Yan - kee	Doo - dle	went	to	town,
1 ne	2 ne	1	ne	2
p c	p c	p	c	p c

It is easily shifted to triple feeling by audiating with the triple syllables and pat-clap-claps:

Yan - kee	Doo - dle	went	to	town,
1 ni	2 ni	1	ni	2
p c c	p c c	p c	c	p c c

Duple and triple meter patterns may be mixed together in the same exercise or song—such as triplets in a basically duple meter piece. Combined meter patterns may only occur with evenly spaced tempo beat feeling.

Songs in duple or triple meter may also be switched to unusual meter feeling by keeping the tempo beats in the same location. The tempo beats become unevenly spaced because the meter beats must be evenly spaced across all groupings. Yankee Doodle could be started as follows:

```
Yan - kee   Doo - dle   went   to    town,
du     bi    du     be    du     bi    du
p    c    c    p        c      p    c    c    p    c
```

Students may make different decisions about how the pattern sounds should be arranged in a new meter. For example, the duple feeling pattern could be changed to triple feeling as follows:

```
1    ne  ta    becomes    1  na  ni    or    1         ta  ni
p    c                     p   c   c           p         c    c
```

There is no absolutely "correct" version. To facilitate meter switching by groups of instrumentalists, assign a few individuals the physical movements for the tempo beats and a few the movements for meter beats while others perform with instruments. A secure sense of meter may be developed by regularly singing and playing familiar tunes in different meter feelings. This technique compensates for the lack of published materials in other than duple meter.

Reading Rhythmic Notation

As previously mentioned, notation for any given rhythm patterns may be introduced when correct syllables are consistently chanted with the sound of the patterns. Rhythm notation then represents the familiar aural vocabulary rather than a mathematical system of note values. Note value names should be used initially as descriptive labels, not music theory information. Knowledge of note value proportionalities and fractionalizations is unnecessary. Familiar songs may be performed which are composed of familiar patterns.

An effective technique for associating symbols with patterns is to use a series of flash cards. Six cards may be made from eight- by thirty-inch tagboard:

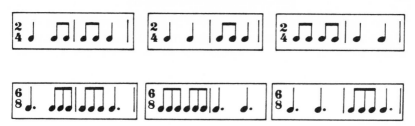

Separate shorter cards should then be made for each of the tempo beat patterns displayed in Figure 4.1. The short cards should be just wide enough to cover the space of one tempo beat on the long cards. It is now possible for the teacher or students to construct many permutations of patterns over four tempo beats duration. The patterns on the cards may be clapped, chanted, and/or performed on given pitches.

Associating symbols with rhythm patterns is expedited through regular written assignments. The mechanics of music notation are first learned by careful copying of familiar tunes and flash card patterns. Home assignments might include copying a portion of the lesson materials, writing familiar patterns in new arrangements, writing the rhythm notation of popular songs, or composing percussion ensembles from multiple lines of rhythm patterns. Students should be expected to perform their own and each other's written work.

Brief dictation tests of familiar rhythm patterns should be a regular part of most lessons. Dictation of familiar rhythm patterns begins with the instructor and students establishing the tempo beat and meter beat feeling with pat-claps. Students should chant the rhythm syllables aloud or silently for the sounded patterns and then write the correct notation. They may then perform their notation with their instruments or by clapping.

Synthesis activities with rhythm notation of familiar tunes and patterns are another important facet of vocabulary development. Students might be requested to locate familiar patterns in their music, to count how many times a particular pattern appears, or to arrange patterns in correct order of a familiar tune. These and other similar activities develop awareness of how melodies are constructed with rhythm patterns.

Meter Signatures

When interpreting meter signatures, the emphasis should be upon what information can be given about rhythmic feeling. The traditional explanation of meter signatures is that the top number refers to how many beats per measure and the lower number refers to the note value which receives one beat. In effect, this is a half-truth. The traditional definition ignores the fact that duple and triple meter signatures indicate different kinds of "beats." If students were knowledgeable about the inconsistencies of the definition, the question would occur immediately, "What kind of beats?" More accurate and meaningful definitions are: duple meter signatures—top numbers are equal to the number of *tempo* beats per measure, lower numbers refer to the note value equal to one *tempo* beat; triple and unusual meter signatures—top numbers are equal to the number of meter beats per measure, lower numbers refer to the note value equal to one meter beat. Students should memorize that top numbers 2 or 4 indicate duple meter feeling; 3, 6, and sometimes 9 or 12 indicate triple meter feeling; 5, 7, 11 and sometimes 9 indicate unusual meter feeling.

Examples of meter signature definitions which provide rhythmic feeling information are listed in Figure 4.3. Notice how each definition provides information about rhythmic feeling rather than just note values.

All patterns with duple feeling are first introduced with two-quarter ($\frac{2}{4}$) meter signatures, and all patterns with triple feeling appear first with six-eighth ($\frac{6}{8}$) meter signatures. Initially it is not sensible or practical to expect instrumental beginners to associate many different symbols with each rhythm feeling concept. In two-quarter meter signature, the tempo beat is visually associated with a quarter note value, and in six-eighth meter signature, the tempo beat is visually associated with the dotted quarter note. The meter beat is associated with the eighth note value in both meter signatures. In these two meter signatures, patterns which coincide with the underlying meter feeling always appear with beamed notation (♫ and ♫♫). This aids visual separation of patterns by tempo beats.

The emphasis in teaching notation is that note values must always represent familiar patterns recognized aurally by their syllable associations. After patterns are known and recognized in two-

The emphasis in teaching notation is that note values must always represent familiar patterns recognized aurally by their syllable associations. After patterns are known and recognized in two-

2 = two tempo beats per measure
4 = a quarter note equals a tempo beat

4 = four tempo beats per measure
4 = a quarter note equals a tempo beat

2 = two tempo beats per measure
2 = a half note equals a tempo beat

2 = two tempo beats per measure
8 = an eighth note equals a tempo beat

4 = four tempo beats per measure
8 = an eighth note equals a tempo beat

Triple Meter Signatures

6 = six meter beats per measure
8 = an eighth note equals a meter beat

3 = three meter beats per measure
8 = an eighth note equals a meter beat

3 = three meter beats per measure
4 = a quarter note equals a meter beat

6 = six meter beats per measure
4 = a quarter note equals a meter beat

Unusual Meter Signatures

5 = five meter beats per measure
8 = an eighth note equals a meter beat

5 = five meter beats per measure
4 = a quarter note equals a meter beat

7 = seven meter beats per measure
8 = an eighth note equals a meter beat

7 = seven meter beats per measure
4 = a quarter note equals a meter beat

Fig. 4.3.   Meter signature definitions.

quarter and six-eighth meter signatures, the same familiar patterns should be symbolically associated with note values in other meter signatures.

The first step when changing to new meter signatures is to move to meter signatures which have new upper numbers but the same lower numbers: four-quarter ($\frac{4}{4}$) for duple feeling and three-eighth ($\frac{3}{8}$) for triple feeling. The net result is a change in the number of bar lines. The note values and syllables are the same as before. For example:

Note that in the duple example every other bar line is removed and in the triple example, twice as many bar lines are needed when the meter signature is changed. In this step, the notation of the patterns does not change, but the number of tempo beats per measure does change. In the duple example, a measure of four-quarter is formed by removing the bar line between two measures of two-quarter. It must be understood that the sound of the patterns remains constant regardless of the number of bar lines. When moving from two to four tempo beats per measure, it is not necessary to count them 1 - 2 - 3 -4. Most students will still see and count the patterns as 1 - 2 - 1 - 2 in each measure regardless of the change in bar lines. Likewise, when moving from six meter beats (two tempo beats) to three meter beats (one tempo beat) per measure, it is not necessary to count each measure as 1 - 1 - 1 - 1. Students tend to group tempo beats in pairs across bar lines as 1 - 2 - 1 - 2 because they hear the patterns with familiar verbal association. Bar lines only change how music looks, not how it sounds.

The next step is to move familiar rhythm patterns into meter signatures with different lower numbers, which changes the notation for the patterns and results visually in a new written "language" for familiar sounds. It is important to recognize again that the syllables for the pattern sounds remain constant regardless of the meter signature. For example:

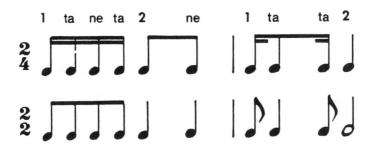

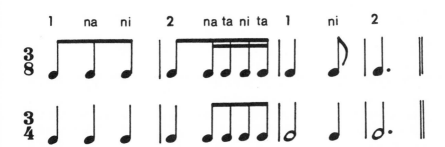

The tempo and meter beat feeling is represented by different note values when the lower number of the meter signature is changed. The sound and the syllables for each pattern remain constant even though the note values are changed. The next duple meter signature to be introduced could be four-eighth ($\frac{4}{8}$), and the next triple meter signature could be six-quarter ($\frac{6}{4}$).

The following example shows how the same set of four melodic rhythm patterns looks when written in four different meter signatures. Again, remember that the syllables for the pattern sounds remain constant regardless of the meter signature.

Changing meter signatures and note values for a rhythm pattern is analogous to changing pitch levels for a tonal pattern. The proportions remain constant among note values for any given rhythm pattern written in two different meter signatures. A new set of flash cards may be constructed for each meter signature so familiar patterns may be practiced with differing notation. Notation for familiar tunes may be translated into new meter signature notation and performed.

Most often, insensitive interpretation results from the use of traditional meter signature definitions as mathematical note value information rather than as an indication of rhythmic feeling. Efficient learning process is ignored when numbers are traditionally used to count tempo beats in duple notation and are used to count meter beats in triple notation. This frequently occurs in beginning method books when students are instructed to count exercises in four-quarter as 1 - 2 - 3 - 4 per measure and exercises in three-quarter as 1 -2 - 3 per measure. Rhythmic feeling is ignored through visually associating numbers with quarter notes regardless of the underlying meter. Songs written in three-quarter are normally felt in one tempo beat per measure and should have numbers associated with tempo beats only. If a song notated in three-quarter is actually felt as three tempo beats per measure, it is no longer triple meter feeling but instead becomes unusual meter with each tempo beat subdivided into duple feeling meter beats. Another typical example is "slow" six-eighth exercises (counted 1 - 2 - 3 - 4 - 5 - 6) and "fast" six-eighth exercises (counted 1 - 2). Almost without exception, all songs written with six-eighth meter signature are felt as two tempo beats per measure. Numbers should only be associated with the two tempo beats and not with the meter beats whenever the tempo is slowed. Songs written in six-eighth may be performed slowly and still be felt with two tempo beats per measure.

Beginning instrumentalists often perform mechanically and without rhythmic feeling (particularly in triple meter) because of the introduction of counting with the notation and use of the same counting association (numbers) with two distinctly different rhythmic feelings (tempo beats and meter beats). The syllable system and rhythm pattern vocabulary advocated in this chapter eliminate this problem with duple and triple counting.

Another misinterpretation of meter signatures occurs when they are associated with how fast or slow an exercise or song is performed. Some method books erroneously imply or instruct that alla breve or "cut time" ($\cent$) is twice as fast as four quarter or common time (c). Meter signatures never indicate tempo. Likewise, note values never indicate speed—sixteenth notes in one song are not necessarily faster than quarter notes in a different song, etc.—but note values do indicate proportionalities within a given exercise or song. The speed of the tempo beat regardless of note values is generally indicated by metronome markings or verbal instructions such as Allegro, Largo, Andante, Presto, and so on.

Contemporary music often includes unusual meter signatures (e.g., $\frac{5}{4}$, $\frac{5}{8}$, $\frac{7}{8}$) where tempo beat feeling is not equally spaced. In order for beginning instrumentalists to gain familiarity and performance skill with unusual meter feeling, it is advisable to experience simple tunes through singing and playing. It is appropriate to introduce unusual meters after a secure foundation in duple and triple meter feeling is established. Songs should first be sung and accompanied with appropriate pat-claps and pat-clap-claps and then attempted with instruments. Troublesome patterns may be isolated and chanted with syllables. Most beginning instrumental materials contain no unusual meter songs. It is possible to switch many songs learned in duple or triple meter to an unusual meter feeling as explained earlier in this chapter. This adds a new dimension of variation and enjoyment to familiar tunes.

Teaching Patterns With Rests

Rests may be systematically introduced when students have acquired a basic vocabulary of rhythm patterns with verbal association. Portions of silence may be incorporated into familiar patterns by echoing patterns and substituting a specified physical movement (such as both hands with palms up) for the rest instead of the corresponding rhythm syllable. Rhythm syllables are not sounded for rests. Rests may be explained as taking the place of certain portions of the sound in familiar patterns or substituting silence for certain sounds.

Rests are particularly easy to introduce in notation. Flash cards for each of the commonly used rest symbols may be placed over corresponding note values on rhythm pattern flash cards. Students should then practice chanting and performing the rhythm patterns from flash cards with rests included. Rhythm syllables should not be chanted for rests. It is often helpful to accompany patterns which include rests with tempo beat and/or meter beat physical movements.

Teaching Dotted Notation

Instrumental music teachers who begin instrument instruction concurrent with notation and without rhythm readiness and vocabulary often delay teaching dotted notation for a number of months. Students are then introduced to dotted notation through explanations of note proportionalities (a dotted quarter note equals three eighth notes, etc.) without rhythmic feeling. Consequently, most students have great difficulty in performing dotted notation accurately.

Conversely, if melodic rhythm patterns are taught initially with syllable associations and no notation, dotted note patterns become no more difficult to learn than any other patterns. Such patterns as D4, D5, D9, and D10 in Figure 4.2 may be introduced in notation whenever students can demonstrate syllable associations for the sound of the patterns. Performance accuracy should always be stressed; teachers should incorporate the movements for the underlying tempo beat and meter beat feeling whenever performance problems occur. It is sometimes helpful to point out how tempo beat or meter beat notation is tied together and sounded as a dotted note. Students can then perform the patterns with rhythmic feeling.

Meter and Conducting Patterns

Conductors of instrumental ensembles often give confusing information to performers when it is unclear whether the beat pattern is coinciding with tempo beat or meter beat feeling. Rhythmic feeling and flow is reinforced when students understand whether the underlying tempo beat or meter beat feeling is conveyed by the conductor. A detailed discussion of this concern may be found in Appendix C.

Other Considerations

Slowing of tempo for practice and rehearsal is a common technique to correct rhythmic problems and to secure difficult passages. Whenever tempos are slowed, it is critical that the underlying tempo and meter beat feelings be maintained. If tempo is slowed so much that the meter beat feeling is changed to tempo beat feeling, a new rhythmic structure occurs, and the melody is no longer felt or performed the same.

Consider the following exercise as a typical example of meter signature practice found in many instrumental method books. It is first intended to be performed with four tempo beats per measure and then with two tempo beats per measure.

This type of exercise may be used but is only appropriate if students understand that 1) the number of tempo beats per measure changes from four to two, 2) the speed of the tempo beats has nothing to do with the meter signature, and 3) that new melodic rhythm patterns are formed by the change of meter signatures while keeping the same notation and that this necessitates different rhythm syllables. The counting for the above exercise in four-quarter would be:

1 2 1 2 / 1 2 1 2 / 1 - 1 - / 1 - 1 - /

The counting for the notation felt in two-half meter signature would be:

1 ne 2 ne / 1 ne 2 ne / 1   2 / 1   2 /

It should be apparent that the verbal association of the rhythm patterns fits with the sound and feeling of the above example regardless of the meter signature or the note value assigned the tempo beat.

Learning syllables and, later, notation for rhythm patterns may be facilitated with practice exercises placed on cassette tapes. A continuous tempo beat sound should be supplied by a metronome while patterns are tapped with a contrasting sound. A usable format is: four tempo beats of patterns, four tempo beats of silence for the student to echo-clap the patterns, four tempo beats while teacher chants the patterns with syllables, four tempo beats of silence for the student to echo-chant the patterns, four tempo beats for the student to play the patterns, four tempo beats rest, new set of patterns begins. After correct syllables can be associated with the sounded rhythm patterns, students should be shown all items in written form with two-quarter meter signature for duple patterns and six-eighth meter signature for triple meter patterns. After the written patterns can be accurately chanted with syllables, the taped items should be taken as a dictation test. The next task is to learn the items in two new meter signatures—two-half for duple and three-quarter for triple. The taped items may now be taken in dictation in the new meter signatures. More meter signature changes may follow.

Improvisation and composition activities with familiar rhythm patterns should be included on a regular basis in lessons and rehearsals. Activities include: changing the melodic rhythm of a familiar tune by performing it with different rhythms, making up simple melodies with a variety of rhythm patterns, composing percussion ensembles, composing percussion accompaniments to melodies, and composing rhythm rounds and ostinatoes.

Little has been said so far concerning the teaching of rhythm theory and notation. This was intentional. Why and how the rhythm system operates as it does becomes meaningful only after functional use. Many teachers insist that students learn proportional note values before performing from notation. Mathematical relationships among note durations are examples of theoretical information of little functional use. Theoretical information abounds in many beginning instrumental materials but, as most students demonstrate, it is of minimal value for developing rhythmic feeling. When the emphasis in teaching and learning rhythm begins with sounds and then a syllable pattern vocabulary, rhythm notation and eventually theory are placed in correct perspective. Theory can then function as a musical experience, not just an academic experience.

Teaching rhythm notation is often complicated by inconsistent editorial practices which allow much music to be published that does not accurately represent intended rhythmic feelings. The four-quarter meter signature is particularly abused. It is used correctly when it indicates four tempo beats per measure, but it is frequently used to notate music that is felt with two tempo beats per measure. It is often necessary when practicing with notation for students and/or teacher first to sing the tune and establish by sound where the tempo beat and meter beat feeling occurs. Then, if needed, they can change the meter signature to fit the correct feeling; for example, without altering notation, a four-quarter meter signature may be changed to two-half, which will indicate the feeling of two tempo beats per measure. Conductors should always be aware of these problems, and as Nilo Hovey points out, "A comparison of meter signature and metronomic indication is always necessary, for they may not agree on the unit of measurement. In this case, the metronome mark should almost always take precedence." [7]

Arrangers of beginning instrumental music often simplify familiar tunes by limiting note values to halves, quarters, and eighths, and by avoiding dotted rhythms. Simplified or "watered down" arrangements avoid supposedly difficult rhythms, but create more problems than are solved. Familiar tunes are best performed as originally learned through singing and listening. Teachers should adjust rhythm notation when necessary to correspond with the version familiar to the students.

Materials

A sense of rhythmic feeling and a rhythm pattern vocabulary are best taught and learned from familiar folk tunes and songs learned in general music classes. Choose materials to correspond with the sequence of patterns to be learned. Written materials should be in the appropriate meter signature sequence. Have students determine tempo beat and meter beat feelings by physical movements and singing if necessary and adjust notation as needed. Student-composed materials may be used extensively. The melodic rhythms of any song may be used as a rhythm round by performing the rhythms on predetermined pitches only, with one or two tempo beat intervals between entries.

It is obvious that the rhythm content of most beginning instrumental method books is designed for teaching symbols of individual note values (whole, half, quarter, eighth, and sixteenth) in order of proportional duration rather than rhythmic feeling and pattern vocabulary. It is undesirable and unnecessary to proceed through method books in the order of the pages. It is always necessary to pick and choose among available materials so needs of individual students may be met and logical rhythm content sequence may be followed.

Rhythm Objectives

The rhythm objectives listed below for instrumentalists incorporate the rhythm content discussed in this chapter with the levels (in parentheses) of the Gordon learning sequence described in chapter 2. The list is intended as an organizational guide for rhythm instruction for beginning instrumentalists regardless of age level. As with the tonal objectives list, sequences of objectives (7-18) are simultaneously overlapped with pattern content differing. Again, the pacing of the overlapped sequences must be determined by the teacher and based upon assessment of student achievement.

The student will be able to:

1.   respond to the sound of music with consistent tempo beat movements (A/O).

2.   respond to the sound of duple meter music with consistent pat-clapping movements (A/O).

3.   respond to the sound of triple meter music with consistent pat-clap-clapping movements (A/O).

4. recognize aurally familiar music without notation as duple or triple meter feeling (A/O).

5. label familiar music as duple or triple meter feeling without notation (VA).

6. label unfamiliar music as duple or triple meter feeling without notation (G).

7. echo-clap/play duple and triple meter melodic rhythm patterns without notation which coincide with underlying tempo and meter beats (A/O).

8. echo-chant duple and triple tempo and meter beat patterns with rhythm syllables and without notation (VA).

9. chant syllables for duple and triple tempo and meter beat patterns after hearing patterns sounded without notation (VA).

10. recognize aurally duple and triple tempo and meter beat patterns in familiar songs without notation (PS). (At this point, overlap objectives by simultaneously beginning a content sequence at number 7 with duple and triple meter patterns which elongate underlying tempo and meter beats or which subdivide meter beats.)

11. recognize aurally duple and triple tempo and meter beat patterns in unfamiliar songs without notation (G).

12. clap/chant/play self-created combinations of familiar duple and triple tempo and meter beat patterns without notation (C/I). (At this point, overlap objectives by simultaneously beginning a content sequence at number 7 with unusual meter melodic rhythm patterns which coincide with underlying tempo and meter beats.)

13. recognize duple and triple tempo and meter beat patterns in notation (SA).

14. clap/chant/play duple and triple tempo and meter beat patterns from notation (SA).

15. recognize, clap/chant/play familiar duple and triple tempo and meter beat patterns within notation of familiar songs (CS).

16. recognize, clap/chant/play familiar duple and triple tempo and meter beat patterns within notation of unfamiliar songs (G). (At this point, overlap objectives by simultaneously beginning a content sequence at number 7 with unusual meter patterns which elongate underlying tempo and meter beats or subdivide meter beats.)

17. improvise, compose, and perform combinations of familiar written duple and triple tempo and meter beat patterns (C/I).

18. understand the theoretical basis for metric function of duple and triple tempo and meter beat patterns (TU).

This list of objectives provides a sequence of rhythm content within a sequence for learning. This is an example of how analysis of content and instructional sequence facilitates diagnostic and prescriptive teaching. The reader is reminded that the process may not necessarily make teaching easier but should make for more effective teaching.

Review Questions

1. What is rhythmic feeling?
2. What is tempo beat feeling?
3. What is meter beat feeling?
4. What are melodic rhythm patterns?
5. Why should beginning instrumentalists develop a rhythm pattern vocabulary?
6. What constitutes the aural/oral level for a sense of rhythmic feeling?
7. What are some activities for developing tempo beat feeling?
8. What are some activities for developing meter beat feeling?
9. Why should beginning instrumentalists work with songs in moderate tempos?
10. How are rhythm patterns taught with verbal association?
11. When and how should beginning instrumentalists be introduced to rhythm notation?
12. What is the rationale for interpreting meter signatures?
13. Why are all duple patterns first notated with two-quarter meter signatures and triple patterns with six-eighth meter signatures?
14. What is the sequence for moving to meter signatures other than two-quarter and six-eighth?
15. How does teaching dotted notation through rhythm patterns differ from the traditional process?
16. What are some of the considerations that often cause difficulties in interpreting rhythm notation with rhythmic feeling?
17. Considering the rhythm pattern 1-ne-ta, what would be an appropriate teaching technique at each level of the Gordon Learning Sequence for beginning instrumentalists?
18. What is the sequence of rhythm content discussed in this chapter?

5

TEACHING TECHNICAL SKILLS
WITH TONAL AND RHYTHMIC CONTENT

THE TWO preceding chapters dealt with teaching of rhythm and tonal concepts in a carefully designed sequence of content and learning skills. The reality of the teaching-learning process with instrumental music is that a sense of tonality, a sense of rhythmic feeling, and technical skills must be taught concurrently on the instruments. Tonal and rhythmic concepts must be stressed with instrumental techniques in lessons and ensemble rehearsals. This chapter contains numerous examples and explanations of how instrumental skills may be acquired and musical results obtained. It is pointless to play an instrument if the results are not musical. James Mursell and Mabelle Glenn comment that, "Our aim in instrumental music must be to teach the instrument through music and for the sake of music, and to use the instrument to refine, define, and make more ardent, the music-making impulse." [1]

It is not the purpose of this chapter to discuss the specific, detailed technical skills required to perform on each instrument. This information is readily available from many sources, and a selected reference list is included at the end of the chapter.

Types of Beginning Instrumental Instruction

Research has provided no conclusive evidence whether private instrumental instruction or class group instruction produces greater musical achievement. Class instruction is the current norm, since it is difficult to justify private lesson instruction in public schools when teacher time and efficiency per student are considered. Beginning class instruction may be found in groups of two to more than seventy. Class groups may comprise like instruments, instrument families, or randomly mixed instruments. Most instrumental teachers, including the author, prefer small group instruction with two to eight students per group. It is preferable for the groups to have like instruments in order to learn musical and instrumental skills efficiently. It is most helpful if students who receive weekly small group instruction also participate weekly in a large ensemble of mixed instruments. The small group lesson allows for more individualized attention to musical and technical needs of students, whereas the large ensemble affords opportunity to experience beginning band and orchestra music with emphasis on ensemble performance skills.

The key to effective class instruction is to meet the differing musical and technical needs of each individual within a group setting. This does not mean attending to one student at a time while the remainder sit and wait for their turn. Developing the musical potential of students requires involvement of the entire class in the learning process without necessarily having everyone do the same task at the same time. Class instruction techniques may also capitalize on peer group learning and motivation. Group performance may be emphasized but must not exclude the development of musical independence and individual student needs.

Instrumental Techniques

Playing a musical instrument requires systematic accomplishment of basic manipulative skills. The types of skills or techniques depend upon the particular instrument to be studied. Typical instrumental techniques include embouchure, bowing, hand positions, breath support, body posture, tonguing, tone quality, fingering patterns, intonation, and vibrato. Many of these techniques overlap and interact on an instrument; for example, tone quality is dependent upon breath support, embouchure, and posture when playing a wind instrument.

Acquiring instrumental technique involves motor control and muscle training in addition to musical skills. Careful practice is necessary to learn how to express musical intent with an instrument.

Frank R. Wilson, a neurologist writing about motor skills and instrumental performance, states:

> Slow practice is the key to rapid technical progress. The cerebellum is a non-judgmental part of the brain; it assumes that any repetitive activity in the muscular system is being repeated because the conscious mind is trying to make it automatic. The cerebellum will be just as efficient an automatizer of incorrect sequences of timing as of those that are correct. When practicing takes place at a pace too fast for accurate playing, there is very little chance for the material to be mastered, and reliable, confident performance simply will not occur. On the other hand, it is probably true that practice for speed is seldom necessary. The cerebellum can supply all the speed wanted if patterning is correct during practice. [2]

Many method book authors and instrumental teachers emphasize extensive technique development with beginning students before considerable melodic material is attempted. Contrived exercises emphasize motor skill development of fingering patterns and bowings. The primary objectives are mechanical rather than musical. This approach is consistent with European music conservatory practices which began in the nineteenth century. Its continued advocacy in many private teaching studios, especially in universities, has influenced many school music instrumental teachers who, in turn, use the same techniques with beginning instrumentalists.

Sequences for introducing instrumental techniques and how the techniques should be taught have evolved over the years. Opinions often vary concerning such issues as the best beginning bow grip, the proportion of upper and lower lips in cup mouthpieces, when to introduce alternate fingerings, or how to teach vibrato. Practical experiences and a minimal research base underlie current practice. Most beginning level instrument instruction books dwell upon technical skills taught with music notation. Some materials introduce a few melodies in conjunction with technical exercises. A few instruction books do emphasize playing melodies without many added technical exercises.

Learning an instrument is much easier when tonal and rhythm pattern vocabularies are first developed in general music classes through singing and chanting. Instrumental teaching can then stress development of instrument skills as a means for expressing the familiar musical vocabulary. Unfortunately, most beginning instrumental students have not had adequate previous music vocabulary training and must be taught tonal and rhythmic content while learning an instrument, a less efficient, though possible, sequence.

Instrumental teachers need to assess the beginning student's prior musical achievement so that appropriate musical instruction may be included with instrumental skills. Information to be gathered about each beginning instrumentalist should include use of singing voice, song repertoire, tonal and rhythmic strengths and weaknesses, and music reading facility. Data should be collected with group achievement tests (standardized and/or teacher-constructed), a standardized music aptitude test, and individual performance tests. Remember, knowing names of music symbols does not constitute functional music achievement. General music teachers may be able to provide much of the information needed; otherwise, the instrumental teacher should schedule time to complete the assessment of the beginner's prior music achievement.

Technical skill development can be logically coordinated with tonal and rhythm pattern vocabulary if the instrument is to be used to express musical ideas. Technical skill as an end in itself, however, merely becomes acrobatics. Students become too easily enamored with how fast their fingers can move or how high a pitch they can play rather than how musically they can perform. Motivation to perform musically is provided through integration of technical demands with musical content. Beginning instrumental instruction is most efficient in producing functional musicians when tonal and rhythmic pattern content is related to melodic materials and is the basis for technical development.

The most important instrumental skill to be developed is pleasing tone quality. Other instrumental skills and musical attempts are not productive if a solid basis for tone production and quality is not established first. Good tone quality is learned best through imitation of live or recorded models of sound rather than verbal or written descriptions. Suzuki (1969) techniques for teaching stringed instruments include extensive listening to recorded lesson materials and also performing without notation. Both techniques are essential to initial development of tone quality.

The first sounds produced on an instrument should not be considered as isolated pitches, but rather, as components of familiar tonal patterns consisting of two to five pitches. Careful attention to skills necessary to produce good tone quality is essential at all times, but the eventual goal is to perform accurate tonal patterns that were previously learned with tonal syllables. These first tonal patterns should be performed without consideration for rhythm and without notation. Emphasis is only directed to accurate pitches with good tone quality in pattern configurations. Correct fingerings should be demonstrated by the teacher and may be labeled with the note names. Extending the range with new fingerings is accomplished by moving the same familiar tonal patterns to new pitch locations. Choice of patterns depends upon tonal pattern content sequence as discussed in chapter 3.

A First Lesson Example

A musical objective for the first lesson on a woodwind instrument could be to teach the familiar patterns M R̲ D̲ and D R̄ M̄. (It is assumed that students can sing the two patterns accurately with tonal syllables.) The two patterns may be performed with left hand fingerings only. Thumb and first finger (T-1) produce *mi*, T-1-2 produce *re*, and T-1-2-3 produce *do*. M R̲ D̲ is easily learned by adding one finger at a time, and D R̄ M̄ by simply removing one finger for each pitch. Students should first hear the teacher perform the patterns and observe the fingerings. A pattern should then be sung with tonal syllables and then sung again with syllables while practicing the fingerings. Performing the patterns with instruments may then begin. Remember that notation and rhythm are not taught at this point. The assignment now is to use the two tonal patterns to play three familiar tunes: "Hot Cross Buns," "Pierrot's Door" (first half), and "Mary Had A Little Lamb." If a student does not know one of the songs, the song must first be learned by rote through singing the words.

Move the patterns and tunes to a new pitch level during the first lesson. It is essential to move them no later than the second lesson so that tonal syllables do not become primarily associated with specific fingerings. It is important to learn that the pitch produced with each fingering may be used for any tonal syllable. A suggested order for woodwinds would be to move next to right hand fingers only while left hand fingers remain down. The fingering pattern for right hand only M R̲ D̲ and D R̄ M̄ varies depending upon which woodwind instrument is used. The patterns may next be moved to a pitch level which requires movement of fingers on both hands, for example, F, G, and A on flute, saxophone, and oboe. Each time the patterns are moved, the teacher should first demonstrate the new fingerings, and students should sing with the syllables while doing the fingerings, perform the patterns with instruments, and then practice the three-note tunes without notation. Introduce whatever correct fingerings are necessary to perform the patterns and tunes. By the second lesson, the same process should begin for teaching D T̲ L̲ and L T̄ D̄ patterns for tonic minor function. The three tunes may be switched to minor mode using the new patterns. Again, move the patterns to different pitch levels as soon as possible. Range expansion and number of fingerings learned will proceed rapidly for most students.

This pattern sequence is directly adaptable to brasses, strings, mallet percussion, and keyboard. Three-valve brasses may begin in mid-range; for example, trumpet: C, D, E, then move to D, E, F-sharp and E, F-sharp, G-sharp. Strings should play the patterns on each string. Keyboard instruments have complete flexibility of pitch location including octaves, and students should be encouraged to utilize the entire keyboard.

The two tonal patterns are initially performed without rhythm pattern interaction. Ordinarily, students will be able to perform the three-note tunes with correct rhythms because they are familiar with them through singing. Consistent tempo beat and meter beat feeling should be stressed while performing the songs. Watch for fingering coordination problems, which cause breakdowns in rhythmic flow. Return to singing the patterns and songs while doing the fingerings whenever necessary.

The advantages of these procedures are many. Musical sound and tone quality are always emphasized first. The student's goal is to produce familiar musical sounds. Learning new fingerings and technical development is facilitated with a minimal tonal pattern vocabulary. Students have musical reasons to use the fingerings and to strive for good sounds. Fingering patterns and coordination are learned without pointless drill activities. Technique becomes an outgrowth of musical practice. A sense of tonality is reinforced through the two tonal patterns in major and two more in minor. Through use of the familiar tunes and tonal patterns, students can remember how they should sound during practice times that are not supervised by the instructor.

It is important to remember that the previous example of content and technique is accomplished without notation. Notation of the patterns and the three-note tunes should be introduced at appropriate pitch levels after students demonstrate their ability to perform the tunes. Names of notes are initially associated with fingerings so pitch levels may be designated (e.g., "Play with do as G."). After learning to perform a tune at a new pitch level, students might be shown the new notation for D R M and M R D and then asked to write out the pitches for the tune (rhythm may or may not be notated, depending on the student's rhythm achievement level).

Rhythm Patterns and Instrument Skills

Familiar rhythm patterns may be used for articulation practice on all instruments. Tonguing or bowing, for instance, can be developed while performing rhythm patterns on given pitches with set tempos. Familiar rhythm patterns should be used without notation. Teachers should always refer to rhythm patterns with correct syllables rather than note values. Verbal instructions, for example, should be, "Play 1 ne ta 2 ne on G," rather than, "Play an eighth-note, two sixteenth-notes and two eighths on G." By giving instructions which refer to rhythmic feeling instead of asking for a given pitch to be performed as a particular written note value, students relate to their rhythm pattern vocabulary. Consistent tempo beat and meter beat feeling should be stressed at all times when students chant or perform rhythm patterns.

A series of wind instrument articulation exercises on a given pitch with four tempo beats per line in a moderate speed might proceed with the teacher instructing the student as follows:

1. Tongue each tempo beat.
2. Tongue on 1 ne 2 ne.
3. Tongue on 1 ta ne ta 2 ta ne ta.
4. Tongue on 1   ne ta 2   ne ta.
5. Tongue on 1 ta ne   2 ta ne.
6. Tongue on 1 na ni 2 na ni.
7. Tongue on 1 ta na ta ni ta 2 ta na ta ni ta.
8. Tongue on 1   na ta ni ta 2   na ta ni ta.
9. Tongue on 1 ta na ta ni   2 ta na ta ni.

The relationship to the underlying rhythmic feeling is established for each of these suggested exercises through verbal reference to the syllables used for the desired pattern and not to note value names. Patterns should be chanted with syllables before performing on the instrument. The speed for each exercise may be gradually increased as students gain proficiency, but the underlying rhythmic feeling remains constant. Tonal interaction is minimized by using only one pitch for the rhythm and articulation practice. The objective for students is to perform a familiar rhythm pattern accurately with precise articulation.

Rhythmic variations of familiar melodies may be performed by changing the melodic rhythm patterns but not the pitches. A rhythmic variation of a melody will not follow the rhythm of the words but will retain the pitch relationships. Articulation and new rhythm patterns may be practiced without the connotations of drill. The following example uses the first line of "Twinkle, Twinkle, Little Star" to show how the entire melodic rhythm might be changed. The tonal syllables change with each tempo beat in this example and are included under the words. The first line of rhythm syllables under the text fits the original version, and the remaining lines are some of the possible melodic rhythm pattern variations:

Twin	-	kle	twin	-	kle		lit	-	tle		star,
Do			So̅				La̅				So̲
1		ne	2		ne		1		ne		2

Duple variations:

1	ta		ne	ta	2	ta	ne	ta	1	ta	ne	ta	2	ta	ne	ta
1	ta			ta	2	ta		ta	1	ta		ta	2	ta		ta
1	ta				2	ta			1	ta			2	ta		
1				ta	2			ta	1			ta	2			ta

Triple variations:

1		ni	2			ni	1		ni	2
1	na		2		na		1	na		2

The melodic rhythm pattern for each tempo beat in the example is performed without altering the tonal outline of the original melody. The same melodic rhythm pattern variations may be repeated throughout the tune, or each phrase could use a different pattern. Tonguing and slurring or bowing patterns may be superimposed upon the rhythm patterns. Students should be encouraged to perform and write down their own rhythmic variations of familiar melodies.

Scales

Scale exercises are included in most instrumental books. Scales are most often taught as fingering or theory exercises rather than tonal or rhythmic studies. Scales are not tonal patterns as defined in chapter 3, but they may be used to develop a sense of tonality. Scales may be sung with tonal syllables before performing with an instrument, and may be divided into segments which are learned as tonal patterns. The ascending major scale could be constructed of D R̄ M̄ F and S L̄ T̄ D̄ or D R̄ M̄ F S̄ and L T̄ D̄ or D R̄ M̄ and F S̄ L̄ T̄ D̄. The ascending harmonic minor scale could be constructed of L $\overline{T}$ $\overline{D}$ R and M $\overline{F}$ $\overline{Si}$ L or L $\overline{T}$ $\overline{D}$ $\overline{R}$ $\overline{M}$ and F $\overline{Si}$ L or L $\overline{T}$ $\overline{D}$ and R $\overline{M}$ $\overline{F}$ $\overline{Si}$ L. The patterns may be learned separately and then connected to build scales in all keys. The student objective is to perform familiar tonal patterns in scale configurations and at the same time, acquire acceptable fingering technique. These same tonal patterns derived from scales become a part of melodic pattern vocabulary when they appear in melodies.

Most instrumental materials emphasize major scales and only a few minor scales. As explained in chapter 3, initial tonal content should include about half major and half minor songs so scale study material should parallel these proportions. Scales should be practiced in all keys for finger facility and range extension. When students can perform songs in modes other than major and minor, corresponding scale studies should eventually be included in all modes. Again, tonal patterns may be used to learn the scales in the new modes. For example, the ascending mixolydian scale could be constructed from S $\overline{L}$ $\overline{T}$ $\overline{D}$ and R $\overline{M}$ $\overline{F}$ $\overline{S}$ or S $\overline{L}$ $\overline{T}$ $\overline{D}$ R and M $\overline{F}$ $\overline{S}$ or S $\overline{L}$ $\overline{T}$ and $\overline{D}$ $\overline{R}$ $\overline{M}$ $\overline{F}$ $\overline{S}$. The ascending dorian scale could be constructed from R $\overline{M}$ $\overline{F}$ $\overline{S}$ and L $\overline{T}$ $\overline{D}$ $\overline{R}$ or R $\overline{M}$ $\overline{F}$ $\overline{S}$ $\overline{L}$ and T $\overline{D}$ $\overline{R}$ or R $\overline{M}$ $\overline{F}$ and S $\overline{L}$ $\overline{T}$ $\overline{D}$ $\overline{R}$. It should become apparent that the same tonal patterns and fingering patterns occur in different combinations to construct various scales. Only the harmonic function of the tonal patterns changes with new scale locations. Students should be able to perform and notate the scales in all modes and in all keys after careful, consistent study. Attention should be drawn to tonal patterns from scales and the related fingering patterns when they occur in melodies.

Rhythm patterns and various articulation patterns may also be combined with scale studies. Each scale degree may be assigned a rhythm pattern or series of patterns to be performed with a given articulation pattern. The objective for the student is now threefold—to perform rhythm patterns, tonal patterns, and articulation patterns accurately.

Diatonic ascending and descending scales may be altered with tonal pattern variations for further study material. Scales in thirds are a common example. Rather than concentrate only on the new fingering patterns, the tonal patterns should be the primary learning goal. An ascending major scale in thirds could be considered as a series of two-tone patterns: D $\overline{M}$, R $\overline{F}$, M $\overline{S}$, F $\overline{L}$, S $\overline{T}$, L $\overline{D}$, plus T $\overline{R}$ $\underline{D}$. A predetermined rhythm pattern and articulation could also be assigned each pitch to add complexity. Arpeggio studies such as those described in chapter 3 in Figures 3.2 and 3.5 are also useful fingering exercises and may be given added difficulty with assigned rhythms and articulations in a variety of keys and modes.

Changing Keys, Modes, and Meters

Transposition occurs whenever a melody is moved to a new pitch level with a corresponding key signature change. Transposition is usually considered to be an advanced technique and then taught as an intervallic and theoretical exercise with notation. The result is that most instrumentalists are not accomplished in transposition. Transposition of melodies is a useful technique for acquiring instrumental technique and expanding ranges. It need not be difficult or advanced if intervals, notation, and theory are initially avoided. Transposition begins in the first lessons without notation by shifting initial tonal patterns and melodies to different starting pitches on the instrument. This allows new fingerings to be learned and range to extend without need for additional material. All students should regularly be expected to move familiar tunes and patterns to different pitch locations without notation. Later, as facility for reading and writing notation develops, students should be expected to write patterns and melodies at various pitch levels. Transposition skills are established by continued practice as new materials are introduced. Eventually, even complex patterns may be performed with minimal difficulty at various pitch levels.

The techniques for changing modes and meters were described in chapters 3 and 4. Musical and technical skills are developed by these techniques. Difficulty and complexity of assignments can be increased by combining key, mode, and meter changes with songs. More advanced students may be challenged while less complex tasks are assigned to less advanced students.

Additional Musical Content

Tonal and rhythmic content can be the basis for developing instrumental technique, and can also be the foundation for additional musical considerations. Specifically, musical style, phrasing, tempos, dynamics, harmony, and form may be taught through tonal and rhythm pattern vocabularies and familiar melodies.

Style training begins with articulation of tonal and rhythm patterns. Staccato, marcato, and legato performance of pitches in patterns and songs should begin with the first few lessons. Familiar songs should be practiced with each articulation style. Phrasing is best introduced through singing the words of songs and then performing with instruments to imitate the sung phrases. It is preferable if all melodies for beginning instrumentalists include the words so that singing of phrases can be easily practiced. The concept of ending phrases where a line of text ends and a breath is normally taken should be taught to all instrumentalists regardless of instrument. The interactions of tempo changes with style and phrasing may also be studied through pattern vocabulary and melodic material.

Beginning instrumentalists should learn to perform their pattern and song repertoire with dynamic contrasts. Although most beginning materials ignore dynamic markings, the concepts of playing soft, medium loud, and loud need to be stressed as soon as acceptable tone quality is produced. More gradations of dynamics including crescendo and decrescendo may be introduced as instrumental skills become more secure. Expressive performance at all levels must include control of dynamics.

The Arpeggio Worksheet included in chapter 3 as Figure 3.5 provides material for performing harmony lines. Rounds, simple duets, partner songs, trios, and quartets are also helpful in developing the awareness of harmonic progressions and lines. Many students are capable of improvising harmony lines to familiar melodies and should be expected to do so without notation. After facility with writing notation has begun, harmony lines may become written assignments. Class lesson groups may compose and perform their own small ensemble arrangements.

Tonal and rhythmic content may also serve as the basis for learning about musical forms. Patterns may be combined and grouped to teach concepts of repetition, contrasting sections, variations, development, etc. Composition assignments may include common forms such as rondo, ABA, AABA, and theme and variations. Students may devise variations of melodies by changing tonal and rhythm patterns, articulations, modes, meters, keys, and so on.

Making Choices

Instrumental technique and musical skills can progress with interest and motivation when students have the opportunity to make use of their musical capabilities. Opportunities for musical growth occur by involving learners in decisions about how many different ways familiar songs may be performed. Some possible choices are displayed in the following list:

Key: C-flat, D-flat, A-flat, E-flat, B-flat, F, C, G, D, A, E, B, F-sharp, C-sharp
Mode: Major, Minor, Dorian, Mixolydian, Phrygian, Lydian
Meter: Duple, Triple, Unusual
Tempo: Slow, Moderate, Fast
Articulation: Legato, Marcato, Staccato
Dynamics: Soft, Medium soft, Medium loud, Loud

Any given melody could be practiced and performed in many combinations of choices taken from the six categories. "Yankee Doodle" is usually first learned in F Major, Duple, Moderate, Marcato, and Medium loud. The song may be used to learn many musical and technical skills by changing one category at a time. Eventually, all categories may change from the original version—D Minor, Triple, Fast, Staccato, and Soft—and the song takes on a new character. After learning a familiar song, students may use the above list to determine what new version to practice. It should not be necessary to notate new versions before performance, but written assignments may be generated with the list. The list should be built gradually as students acquire facility in each category. Songs should be taken through as many combinations of categories as are practical and of interest to students. The objective for the students is to function with their musical and technical skills through musical manipulation of familiar songs.

Rehearsal Warmups

The first few minutes of ensemble rehearsals and class lessons should be devoted to warmup activities. Hovey states that the purposes of ensemble warmup procedures are: "(1) to bring the instrument to the temperature (and hence the pitch level) of normal playing, (2) to prepare the players' embouchures, and also correct reed placement and response, (3) to provide ear-training and encourage careful listening, (4) to develop good ensemble playing habits, and (5) to establish a mental set conducive to a successful rehearsal." [3] The primary objective of a warmup period should be to stress musical skills and instrumental techniques. Too often, warmup time becomes only an attempt to blow warm air through horns, scratch with a bow, or pound with mallets while carelessly playing up and down a scale. Content for warmup activities should center around tonal and rhythmic pattern vocabularies. The six categories of Key, Mode, Meter, Tempo, Articulation, and Dynamics provide a variety of musical considerations to be included in warmups. Scale exercises should also be performed with content from the category list. Material should be performed within comfortable ranges.

Acceptable instrumental techniques and accurate ensemble playing should also be stressed during warmups. Tone quality, posture, fingerings, and so forth, need continual attention by performers and instructor. Ensemble concerns of blend, balance, precision, and intonation should also be addressed during warmup activities. Intonation training is directly related to a sense of tonality and correct instrumental techniques. Simple chord progressions and chorales offer much opportunity for musical learning in ensemble rehearsals directed by discerning educator-conductors.

Diagnosis and Prescription

Instrumentalists must attend to many variables in order to function and perform musically. Effective teachers must be able to diagnose and correct instrumental performance problems when they occur. The teacher must first discern that a problem exists, then determine specifically what the problem is, and last decide what to do and how to make corrections. Diagnosis is facilitated by organizing possible problems into two categories—instrumental technique and musical content. Each category may be subdivided into various components. Appropriate level of learning sequence must be determined as it interacts with musical content. Materials and teaching techniques are then chosen which are used to solve the performance problem. Efficiency of teaching/learning and chances for student success improve greatly when teachers apply an organizational structure to problem solving rather than random, nonsystematic techniques. Diagnostic and prescriptive teaching should gain effectiveness through continued teaching experience.

In the following chart, the Diagnosis section contains two columns. The column on the left displays categories for labeling most common instrumental performance errors in musical content and instrument technique. The middle column lists the learning sequence for use with tonal and rhythm patterns when diagnosing problems. The Prescription column would be filled in by the teacher with appropriate materials, teaching techniques, and activities to meet the diagnosed needs of individual students or classes.

	Diagnosis	*Prescription*
(problem is due to:)	(where in learning sequence)	(appropriate materials and teaching technique)
Musical Content	Aural/Oral	
Tonal or Rhythmic	Verbal association	
Key	Partial synthesis	
Mode	Symbolic association	
Meter	Composite synthesis	
Tempo	Generalization	
Artic, style	Creativity/Improvisation	
Dynamics	Theoretical Understanding	

Instrumental Technique

   Tone Quality
   Embouchure
   Bowing
   Posture and holding position
   Breath Support
   Tonguing
   Finger Technique
   Intonation and Tuning

The musical content and instrumental techniques listed above are not intended to be all-inclusive, but rather to provide broad classifications which cover most instrumental performance errors. Diagnosis includes determination of the problem, and in the case of rhythm or tonal errors, what level of learning sequence is involved. In order to think diagnostically, rhythm and tonal content sequence within the learning sequence must be followed. Logical ordering of prerequisites is essential for effective prescriptive content and techniques. Instrument techniques and musical content continuously interact. Instrument techniques are developed as a result of the musical content sequence, and musical content may be chosen to teach specific instrument techniques.

Learning Sequence and Diagnosis/Prescription

Using the Gordon skills learning sequence can be an efficient means to diagnose tonal and rhythmic pattern learning problems and to prescribe the next appropriate task. The learning skills level for any given tonal or rhythmic pattern is readily assessed. Knowledge of the sequence then permits effective choice of the succeeding step for the student. The following examples list a teaching activity at each learning sequence level for a given pattern to be taught:

Rhythm pattern

Aural/Oral—teacher claps pattern, student echo-claps
Verbal Association—teacher chants pattern, student echo-chants
Partial Synthesis—student aurally recognizes pattern in a familiar song
Symbolic Association—student sees pattern on a flash card and chants syllables
Composite Synthesis—student visually recognizes pattern in a familiar song
Generalization—student aurally or visually recognizes pattern in an unfamiliar song
Creativity/Improvisation—student includes the pattern in a rhythmic improvisation or composition
Theoretical Understanding—student learns the proportionality of note values within the pattern

Tonal Pattern

Aural/Oral—teacher sings pattern on lu, student echo-sings/plays
Verbal Association—teacher sings pattern with syllables, student echo-sings/plays
Partial Synthesis—student aurally recognizes pattern in a familiar song
Symbolic Association—student sees the pattern on a flash card and sings and/or plays it
Composite Synthesis—student visually recognizes pattern in a familiar song
Generalization—student aurally or visually recognizes the pattern in an unfamiliar song
Creativity/Improvisation—student utilizes the pattern in a composition
Theoretical Understanding—student learns the interval names within the pattern

Creativity/Improvisation—student utilizes the pattern in a composition

Theoretical Understanding—student learns the interval names within the pattern

If a student is unable to perform a pattern at any given sequence level, the teacher should drop back one step before moving forward again. Appropriate teaching techniques should be chosen for each level. The pacing and timing of moving from level to level will vary with individual students. It should not be expected or demanded that all students in a group do the same activity level at the same time. Students should play patterns as soon as they can consistently demonstrate correct verbal associations with syllables. Patterns should be performed at different pitch levels.

An example of procedures which incorporate learning sequence skills for a student who has trouble performing a written passage of music is:

1.   Without notation, the student echoes the teacher by singing the correct pitches using the words of the song or a neutral syllable such as "lu" (A/O) and then uses moveable *do* syllables without the rhythm (VA).

2.   Student sings the passage from notation while doing the fingerings without the rhythm (SA).

3.   Student plays the passage without rhythm from notation with emphasis on correct intonation, tone production, and fingerings (SA). (The teacher may relate the passage to appropriate chord arpeggios or provide chordal accompaniment.)

4.   Student chants rhythm syllables of the passage with consistent tempo beat feeling (SA). If needed, revert to echo-chanting the patterns without notation before proceeding (VA).

5.   Student performs fingerings in correct rhythm without sound (SA).

6.   Student performs the passage with correct tone production, intonation, fingerings, articulations, and rhythm (CS).

Class Lesson Example

This approximately forty-minute lesson is designed for a class of first-year clarinetists. It is intended as an example for the reader to follow the combining of tonal and rhythmic content with instrumental techniques. Prior to this lesson, the class has learned to read some familiar songs. No new rhythm patterns are presented in this lesson; however, some of the tonal patterns have not occurred previously for the class in this key. Teaching objectives of the lesson are:

1. To review and/or learn the tonal patterns as listed in D major.
2. To review the rhythm patterns as listed.
3. To develop facility to finger A by rolling the left hand first finger.
4. To change a familiar duple meter song to triple feeling.
5. To change a familiar major song to minor mode.

Material: Song Worksheet #1   "Lightly Row"

Lesson chronology:
—assemble instruments, check for workable reeds
—warmup with D R̄ M̄ F̄ S̄, D M̄ S̄, S M̲, F R̲ (echo-sing, check A fingering facility)
—sing through the song ("Is it a D M̄ S̄ or L D̄ M̄ song?" "Is it duple or triple feeling?")
—sing through the song while doing fingerings, make corrections as needed
—play song (check A fingering facility)
—sing song again while doing fingerings, if necessary
—practice tonal patterns again if A fingering needs work
—find tonal patterns in the notation
—"Can anyone name other familiar songs that contain any of these tonal patterns?"
—sing song in minor (teacher gives i-V$_7$-i introduction and chordal accompaniment)
—sing/play L T̄ D̄ R̄ M̄, L D̄ M̲,M D̲, R T̲ in D minor
—play song in D minor ("What fingerings changed from the major version?")
—establish p-c-c feeling and sing/play in triple major
—sing in triple minor while doing fingerings
—play in triple minor
—Assignment — next week perform "Lightly Row" and the tonal patterns in two new keys of your choice in duple and triple feeling. Practice one of the new versions with staccato articulation and the other with legato articulation. Write out the new versions in each key. Perform any song or excerpt which uses some of the same tonal patterns.

SONG WORKSHEET #1

LIGHTLY ROW Key______ Mode______ Meter______

Rhythm Patterns:

Tonal Patterns: S M, F R, D R M F S, D M S, R M F, M F S, S D

Assignments:

Change to triple feeling

Change to minor mode

Write out and perform in the Keys of ____________________

____

____

____

Fig. 5.1. Model for a song worksheet.

The lesson example centers around musical content while developing fingering facility. Learning sequence is followed by moving from aural/oral activities through synthesis and generalization. Opportunities exist for class members to be doing different tasks simultaneously such as singing, fingering, playing, and recognizing patterns. Rhythm problems are avoided by presenting only familiar patterns.

Whenever students are expected to practice unsupervised at home, it is essential that lesson activities prepare for effective practice. Success in home practice is encouraged by assigning a familiar song but adding new technical and musical demands. It is wise to determine the learning sequence level asked of students in weekly assignments and make certain that prerequisites are accomplished. During instrumental lessons, musical preparations for the succeeding lesson should take place so that home practice during intervening days may concentrate on smoothing out instrument technique problems.

Materials

Lesson materials for beginning instrumentalists should be chosen with tonal and rhythmic patterns in mind. As was mentioned in previous chapters, simple folk songs and general music repertoire are most appropriate. Many teachers rely primarily upon trite, contrived exercises from instrument method books. Good teaching demands finding materials which fit the content objectives. It is not productive to choose a beginning instrument book and follow through it page by page under the assumption that the content is efficiently organized and appropriate for learning.

All students should work on song material which includes independent parts. Ostinatos, harmony lines, combinable sections, partner songs, and rounds are particularly useful in developing independent performers. Class lessons and ensemble rehearsals should include materials to be performed in parts. Early attention to blend, balance, tone quality, intonation, articulations, and rhythmic accuracy then becomes possible.

Sightreading (generalization at the symbolic association level) materials should be introduced soon after students can read and perform some familiar songs. Unfamiliar songs which include familiar tonal and rhythmic patterns should be chosen for sightreading material. The author recommends choosing material with at least seventy-five percent familiar patterns. Unfamiliar patterns which students can not perform should be echoed with correct syllables before attempting them again in notation.

Solo literature and small ensemble music are an integral part of materials to develop instrumental musicians. Interesting and worthwhile selections are available from the beginning level on for all instruments and most ensemble combinations. Solo and small ensemble instruction could become the main musical learning and performance vehicle after beginning class instruction. The main goal for more advanced instrumentalists is expressive and stylistic interpretation of the literature for their instrument.

Students who have developed a tonal and rhythm pattern vocabulary along with instrument facility can also generate many of their own materials. Arranging and composing for instrument classes and ensembles allows students to utilize their musical and instrumental skills in creative and productive ways.

It is important to have regular use and review of materials which require all fingerings and techniques learned. A variety of keys, modes, and meters in material will aid musical and technical skill development.

Review Questions

1. How do class instruction teaching techniques differ from those used in private lessons?

2. How does a vocabulary of tonal and rhythm patterns benefit learning to play an instrument?

3. How can instrument techniques be improved through learning transposition?

4. When and how should training begin for musical style, phrasing, dynamics, and form?

5. How may rehearsal warmups develop instrumental and musical skills?

6. What is the relationship between diagnostic and prescriptive teaching and content and learning sequences?

7. What should be the next step if a student is unable to play a given tonal pattern on a flash card?

8. How should students be prepared for home practice?

9. Examine any beginning instrument book. What are the tonal, rhythmic, and instrument technique sequences?

10. When is it appropriate to begin sightreading activities?

For Further Reading

Woodwinds:

Pence, Homer. *Teacher's Guide to the Bassoon.* Elkhart: Selmer, Inc., 1963.

Putnik, Edwin. *The Art of Flute Playing.* Evanston: Summy-Birchard Co., 1970.

Spencer, William G. *The Art of Bassoon Playing.* 2d ed., revised by Frederick A. Mueller. Evanston: Summy-Birchard Co., 1969.

Sprenkle, Robert and David Ledet. *The Art of Oboe Playing.* Evanston: Summy-Birchard Co., 1961.

Stein, Keith. *The Art of Clarinet Playing.* Evanston: Summy-Birchard Co., 1958.

Teal, Larry. *The Art of Saxophone Playing.* Evanston: Summy-Birchard Co., 1963.

Timm, Everett L. *The Woodwinds: Performance and Instructional Techniques.* 2d ed. Boston: Allyn and Bacon, 1971.

Westphal, Frederick W. *Guide to Teaching Woodwinds.* 2d ed. Dubuque: Wm. C. Brown, 1974.

Woodwind Anthology. Evanston: The Instrumentalist Co., 1972.

Brasses:

Bellamah, Joseph L. *A Survey of Modern Brass Teaching Philosophies.* San Antonio: Southern Music Co., 1976.

Brass Anthology. Evanston: The Instrumentalist Co., 1969.

Brown, Merrill. *Teaching the Successful High School Brass Section.* West Nyack, N.J.: Parker Publishing Co., 1981.

Farkas, Philip. *The Art of Brass Playing.* Bloomington: Brass Publications, 1962.

Farkas, Philip. *The Art of French Horn Playing.* Evanston: Summy-Birchard Co., 1956.

Fink, Reginald. *The Trombonist's Handbook.* Athens, OH: Accura Music, 1977.

Gregory, Robin. *The Horn.* Rev. ed. New York: Frederick A. Praeger, 1969.

Hunt, Norman J. *Guide to Teaching Brass.* Dubuque: Wm. C. Brown Co., 1968.

Johnson, Keith. *The Art of Trumpet Playing.* Ames: The Iowa State Univ. Press, 1981.

Kleinhammer, Edward. *The Art of Trombone Playing.* Evanston: Summy-Birchard Co., 1963.

Sherman, Roger. *The Trumpeter's Handbook.* Athens, OH: Accura

Music, 1979.

Winslow, Robert W. and John E. Green. *Playing and Teaching Brass Instruments.* Englewood Cliffs: Prentice-Hall, Inc., 1964.

Strings:

Galamian, Ivan. *Principles of Violin Playing and Teaching.* Englewood Cliffs: Prentice-Hall, Inc., 1962.

Green, Elizabeth A. H. *Teaching Stringed Instruments in Classes.* Englewood Cliffs: Prentice-Hall, Inc., 1966.

Krolick, Edward. *Basic Principles of Double Bass Playing.* Washington, D.C.: Music Educators' National Conference, 1957.

Lamb, Norman. *Guide to Teaching Strings.* 2d ed. Dubuque: Wm. C. Brown Co., 1976.

Oddo, Vincent. *Playing and Teaching the Strings.* Belmont, CA: Wadsworth Publishing Co., 1979.

Potter, Louis. *The Art of Cello Playing.* Evanston: Summy-Birchard Co., 1964.

Percussion:

Bartlett, Harry R. *Guide to Teaching Percussion.* Dubuque: Wm. C. Brown Co., 1961.

Blades, James. *Orchestral Percussion Technique.* London: Oxford Univ. Press, 1961.

Collins, Myron D. and John E. Green. *Playing and Teaching Percussion Instruments.* Englewood Cliffs: Prentice-Hall, Inc., 1962.

Payson, Al, and Jack McKenzie. *Music Educator's Guide to Percussion.* New York: Belwin, Inc., 1966.

Percussion Anthology. Evanston: The Instrumentalist Co., 1980.

Spohn, Charles. *The Percussion.* 2d ed. Boston: Allyn and Bacon, Inc., 1967.

Music Lists:

Anderson, Paul G. *Brass Ensemble Music Guide.* Evanston: The Instrumentalist Co., 1978.

Anderson, Paul G. *Brass Solo and Study Material Music Guide.* Evanston: The Instrumentalist Co., 1976.

Band Music Guide. Evanston: The Instrumentalist Co.

Selective Music Lists—1978: Full Orchestra, String Orchestra. Washington, D.C.: Music Educators' National Conference, 1978.

Selective Music Lists—1979: Instrumental Solos and Ensembles. Washington, D.C.: Music Educators National Conference, 1979.

Voxman, Himie and Lyle Merriman. *Woodwind Music Guide: Ensemble Music in Print.* Evanston: The Instrumentalist Co., 1982.

Voxman, Himie and Lyle Merriman. *Woodwind Solo and Study Material Guide*. Evanston: The Instrumentalist Co., 1982.

6
ASSESSMENT OF MUSIC ACHIEVEMENT AND MUSIC APTITUDE

THE PRIMARY purpose of schools is to promote cognitive learning, which includes perception, conception, and intuition. The music learning process should result in acquiring knowledge and skills. When instrumental music is included in school curricula, it should be expected that music knowledge and skills are reinforced and acquired through the use of musical instruments. These musical knowledges and skills become the objectives of the instrumental music program and also become the basis for evaluation. If musical objectives are important enough to teach, and if this teaching results in observable student outcomes, measurement is possible and necessary.

Systematic measurement of instrumental music achievement is necessary and desirable for a number of reasons. Probably the most important reason is to assess student progress. Music achievement levels of students need frequent assessment so that appropriate choices of content, materials, and learning levels can be made. Assignment of new tasks should depend upon completion of prerequisite tasks. Instrumental music students whose assignments consist of moving through a method book from page one to the end and then beginning the next book are not being diagnosed or taught effectively. Diagnostic and prescriptive teaching depends upon objective measurement. Teachers need to report music achievement regularly to students and parents, and objective measurement is essential for valid reports. Reporting music achievement must consist of more than a letter grade for music; it should also include an evaluation of skills and objectives, a diagnosis of problem areas, and a prescription for improvement in trouble areas. In addition, evaluation is helpful in that instrumental music teachers may evaluate their own effectiveness through measuring the achievements of their students.

Systematic assessment of music aptitude (potential to achieve musically) is also desirable. Aptitude test results are important for diagnosis of musical strengths and weaknesses and for identifying talented students before training occurs. Low music aptitude test scores should never be a basis for denying instrumental instruction to students. High music aptitude scores are an indication that a student may profit from instrumental music instruction.

Evaluation is the process of making judgments based upon collected data, and measurement is the process of collecting that data. For evaluation to be meaningful, measurement should be objective and systematic; for evaluation to be useful, interpreted data must be reported in some meaningful form.

This chapter will be concerned with describing measurement and evaluation of instrumental music achievement and aptitude. Objectives for instrumental music achievement include achievement outcomes for musical knowledge and skills. Measurement of the tonal and rhythmic content described in previous chapters focuses on the musical component. The instrument component includes the objectives and measurement pertaining to the development of performance technique and knowledge of any given instrument. Selected standardized tests for music achievement and for music aptitude are also discussed.

Measuring Instrumental Music Achievement

Measurement of music achievement is dependent upon clearly understood objectives. The result of teaching carefully planned objectives should be measurable outcomes. Unless both teacher and student understand what the objectives are, measurement is meaningless. Sequential lists of content objectives are most helpful in structuring the teaching and learning process. The content objectives also become the basis for measurement and reporting of achievement. The interaction of learning sequence and content may be stated in objectives by including what is being learned and how students demonstrate their achievement.

Instrumental music teachers often do not take the time necessary to measure student achievement objectively. Many teachers have had little or no training in development or use of measurement tools. School instrumental teachers sometimes think primarily of the achievement levels of large performing groups rather than of the individuals within the groups. They ignore objective measurement of individual musical and skill achievement levels. There are many ways to assess instrumental music achievement systematically. It is essential that teachers learn how to measure objectively and consistently.

Measurement Tools

The most important measurement tools in instrumental music teaching are the teacher's and the students' ears. In addition to hearing music as it is performed, however, teachers and students must learn to analyze and critique what is heard. It must not be assumed that students automatically determine their own weaknesses and strengths. Problems must be diagnosed and corrective techniques and materials prescribed. Ears must be trained to measure music achievement systematically. Ear training in instrumental music is dependent upon development of audiation through a pattern vocabulary, a sense of tonality and meter, and models of sound. The previous chapters in this book have dealt with these topics in detail.

Instrumental performance achievement is measured through aural or visual observation techniques. Both should be as systematic and objective as possible. Aural observation—critical listening—of performance sounds may be done by the teacher and the students. Music teachers should generally listen to student performances with error detection and prescription in mind. Students may be taught to listen carefully to themselves and to each other and give constructive comments.

Visual observation of instrumental performance is used to assess what is physically being accomplished to produce the music. This is a primary measurement practice for instrumental technique objectives, and is most effective when teachers and students observe themselves and each other and give constructive suggestions for improvement.

Objectivity of aural and visual observation of performance achievement can be improved and systematized through use of rating scales. Rating scales may be constructed which fit any performance objective. The simplest form of rating scales is the checklist. A checklist contains a series of statements, which when applied to performance, are determined as accomplished satisfactorily or unsatisfactorily. A point may be awarded for each statement achieved. An example of such a checklist follows:

Minor Tonic Arpeggios Checklist

(check each key when L D M D L is performed accurately)

A minor	
D minor	E minor
G minor	B minor
C minor	F-sharp minor
F minor	C-sharp minor
B-flat minor	G-sharp minor
E-flat minor	D-sharp minor
A-flat minor	A-sharp minor

Another useful form of rating scale is constructed from five criteria statements in a continuum. For example:

Intonation Rating Scale

The overall intonation of the performance was
        5 - superior
        4 - excellent
        3 - average
        2 - fair
        1 - poor

This scale allows for considerable subjectivity on the part of the rater. Standards will vary among raters for any given performance, and individual raters may not be consistent among different performances.

Rating scale subjectivity is minimized when the five criteria statements in the continuum are specific to content objectives. The performance task for the following rating scale example is for the student to chant rhythm syllables in tempo for a series of four rhythm patterns. Pattern content should fit what has been studied. The test patterns should be tape-recorded to eliminate performance errors.

Rhythm Syllable Rating Scale

> 5 - no syllable errors
> 4 - errors in one pattern
> 3 - errors in two patterns
> 2 - errors in three patterns
> 1 - errors in four patterns

This rating scale allows the rater to be objective from student to student. Additional raters using the same scale should also obtain similar results. The scale could also be adapted for use with tonal patterns.

Objectivity of rating scales may often be improved if they are used with tape-recorded performances rather than during the performance. This eliminates distracting visual observations during test performance which may influence rater consistency. Students in class lessons and rehearsals may individually leave the room to tape record a test performance in a separate recording location. The instructor may then listen to the tape at a later time and use appropriate rating scales to measure the performances.

A recommended measurement technique for instrumental performance which uses rating scales is: three brief unfamiliar musical excerpts (approximately eight measures each) of teacher-composed material are selected. The excerpts are of the same difficulty level, and are based upon current achievement of the students to be tested. Excerpt 1 is given to students one week before the test date for home preparation without assistance. Excerpt 2 is given to students one week before the test date for preparation with teacher help. Excerpt 3 is sightread during the testing period. All test performances are tape-recorded. The teacher then listens to the tapes and rates the performances using rating scales which reflect current teaching objectives and content. More than one rating scale may be applied to each performance, such as tonal patterns, consistent tempo, or tone quality. It is best to listen to the taped performances once for each rating scale used. The procedure takes minimal teacher time per student and results in useful measurement data. If used at the end of each grade period (six, nine, twelve, or eighteen weeks) during the school year, student performance progress is objectively documented.

Many varieties of teacher-made test may also be used to measure instrumental music achievement. Multiple choice, matching, and completion tests are particularly appropriate forms for testing cognitive knowledge. Typical content would include: musical terms, composers, composition titles, historical information, key signatures, meter signatures, music theory, and instrument care. Written tests may be used on a regular basis to collect data related to content objectives.

A most useful type of teacher-made test is one in which items require students to respond to musical examples. Tape-recorded musical examples may be constructed to test student musical perception and knowledge. Each item should include two to four response options. This type of item is especially useful for testing mode and meter recognition and for pattern vocabulary association with syllables and notation. Taped items may also be used to test student ability to echo patterns correctly with instruments and for dictation tests.

Measuring Objectives

The final sections of chapters 3 and 4 contained lists of objectives for tonal and rhythm content. The content sequence of the objective lists is repeated below. Tonal and rhythm content enclosed in parentheses within objective statements may be changed as needed to fit the tonal or rhythm content sequences described in chapters 3 and 4; major and minor could be changed to dorian and mixolydian, for example, or duple and triple could be changed to unusual meter; tonic could be changed to dominant-seventh; tempo and meter beat patterns could be changed to subdivision or elongation patterns, and so on. Combining different content lists of objectives through overlapping as indicated in chapters 3 and 4 is not included. Both content and learning sequences are incorporated in the tonal and rhythm lists. In addition, lists of objectives for technical skills of instrument families are included.

A measurement technique (labeled MT) follows each of the objective statements listed here. Each measurement technique is a suggestion pertaining to collection of data relative to student achievement for that particular objective. Many other techniques may also be employed. Teachers may use measurement techniques in formal testing situations where collected data is recorded or in informal achievement assessment during the course of instruction.

Tonal Objectives and Measurement Techniques

Student will be able to:

1. sing/play familiar major and minor songs without notation.
MT: teacher aurally assesses individual performances of assigned songs performed without notation.

2. sing/play major and minor tonic arpeggios with syllables but without notation.
MT: teacher assesses individual performances of assigned tonic arpeggios.

3. recognize aurally major and minor resting tones.
MT: students listen to taped test items of short unfamiliar songs with three ending choices, choose which response ends on the resting tone.

4. label familiar songs as major or minor mode after hearing or performing without notation.
MT: students listen to and identify taped test items of phrases from familiar songs with three response choices: major, minor, other.

5. label unfamiliar songs as major or minor mode after hearing without notation.
MT: students listen to and identify taped test items of phrases from unfamiliar songs with three response choices, major, minor, other.

6. echo-sing/play major and minor tonic function tonal patterns without syllables or notation.
MT: teacher listens to individuals echo-sing/play ten patterns each and records number of patterns echoed accurately.

7. echo-sing major and minor tonic function tonal patterns with tonal syllables and without notation.
MT: teacher listens to individuals echo-sing ten patterns each and records number of patterns echoed with correct tonal syllables and accurate intonation.

8. sing major and minor tonic function tonal patterns with tonal syllables after hearing patterns performed without notation or syllables.
MT: teacher plays patterns and records number of patterns sung accurately with syllables.

9. recognize aurally major and minor tonic function tonal patterns in familiar songs without notation.
MT: teacher asks students to audiate a familiar song and to write which words in the song correspond to previously specified patterns, such as S $\overline{\text{D}}$ $\overline{\text{M}}$.

10. recognize aurally major and minor tonic function tonal patterns in unfamiliar songs without notation.

MT: teacher performs an unfamiliar song and student raises hand whenever previously specified pattern, such as D $\overline{\text{M}}$ $\overline{\text{S}}$, occurs.

11. sing with syllables and play self-created combinations of familiar major and minor tonic function tonal patterns without notation.

MT: teacher rates accuracy of student assignment to choose any six familiar tonal patterns, combine them without notation, sing them with syllables, and then perform them.

12. recognize familiar major and tonic function tonal patterns in notation.

MT: teacher performs selected familiar patterns from ten tonal pattern flashcards, and students respond by indicating which flashcard was performed.

13. sing with syllables, write, and play noted major and minor tonic function tonal patterns.

MT: a) teacher provides notation of familiar patterns on flashcards and records accuracy of student responses of singing with tonal syllables or performing on instruments; b) teacher performs familiar patterns for students to write with correct notation.

14. recognize, sing/play familiar major and minor tonic function tonal patterns within notation of familiar songs.

MT: teacher performs selected familiar patterns from a specific song. While observing the notation for the song, students respond by circling the performed patterns.

15. recognize, sing/play familiar major and minor tonic function tonal patterns within notation of unfamiliar songs.

MT: a) teacher performs selected familiar patterns from an unfamiliar song. While observing the notation for an unfamiliar song, students respond by circling the performed patterns. b) While observing the notation for an unfamiliar song, students are tested by how many familiar tonal patterns they can recognize and perform.

16. improvise, compose, and perform combinations of familiar written major and minor tonic function tonal patterns.

MT: a) teacher rates student improvised variations of familiar written songs; b) teacher rates student written composition assignments; c) teacher rates student performances of compositions.

17. understand the theoretical basis for harmonic function of major and minor tonic function tonal patterns.

MT: students take written test on knowledge of scale and chord writing.

Rhythm Objectives and Measurement Techniques

Student will be able to:

1.   respond to the sound of familiar music with consistent tempo beat movements.

MT: teacher observes student accuracy in responding to tempo beats with patting movements while listening to songs.

2.   respond to the sound of duple meter music with consistent pat-clapping movements.

MT: teacher observes student accuracy in responding to duple meter songs with pat-clapping on meter beats.

3.   respond to the sound of triple meter music with consistent pat-clap-clapping movements.

MT: teacher observes student accuracy in responding to triple meter songs with pat-clap-clapping on meter beats.

4.   recognize aurally familiar music without notation as duple or triple meter feeling.

MT: teacher provides taped excerpts of familiar songs in duple or triple meter feelings. Students decide whether or not the songs fit the pat-clap or pat-clap-clap movements and circle p - c, p - c - c, or *other* for each item on an answer sheet.

5.   label familiar music as duple or triple meter feeling without notation.

MT: students listen to taped test items of phrases from familiar songs in duple, triple, and unusual meters and choose meter type and label from three response options, *duple, triple, other.*

6.   label unfamiliar music as duple or triple meter feeling without notation.

MT: students listen to taped test items of phrases from unfamiliar songs in duple, triple, and unusual meters and choose meter type and label from three response options, *duple, triple, other.*

7.   echo-clap/play duple and triple meter melodic rhythm patterns without notation that coincide with underlying tempo and meter beats.

MT: teacher listens to individuals echo-clap/play ten patterns each and records number of patterns echoed accurately.

8.   echo-chant duple and triple tempo and meter beat patterns with rhythm syllables and without notation.

MT: teacher listens to individuals echo-chant ten patterns each and records number of patterns echoed with correct rhythm syllables and consistent meter feeling.

9.   chant syllables for duple and triple tempo and meter beat

patterns after hearing patterns sounded without syllables or notation.

MT: teacher claps patterns and records number of patterns chanted accurately with syllables.

    10.   recognize aurally duple and triple tempo and meter beat patterns in familiar songs without notation.

MT: teacher asks students to audiate a familiar song and to write which words in the song correspond to previously specified patterns, such as 1 ta ne ta.

    11.   recognize aurally duple and triple tempo and meter beat patterns in unfamiliar songs without notation.

MT: teacher performs an unfamiliar song and student raises hand whenever a previously specified pattern, such as 1 ne ta, occurs.

    12.   clap/chant/play self-created combinations of familiar duple and triple tempo and meter beat patterns without notation.

MT: teacher rates accuracy of student assignment to choose any six familiar rhythm patterns, combine them without notation, chant them with syllables, and perform them.

    13.   recognize duple and triple tempo and meter beat patterns in notation.

MT: teacher performs selected familiar patterns from ten rhythm pattern flashcards. Students respond by indicating which pattern was performed.

    14.   clap/chant/play duple and triple tempo and meter beat patterns from notation.

MT: teacher provides notation of familiar patterns on flashcards and records accuracy of student responses of clapping, chanting, and/or playing.

    15.   recognize, clap/chant/play familiar duple and triple tempo and meter beat patterns within notation of familiar songs.

MT: teacher performs selected familiar patterns from a specific song. While observing the notation for the song, students respond by circling the performed patterns.

    16.   recognize, clap/chant/play familiar duple and triple tempo and meter beat patterns within notation of unfamiliar songs.

MT: teacher performs selected familiar patterns from an unfamiliar song. While observing the notation for the unfamiliar song, students respond by circling the performed patterns.

    17.   improvise, compose, and perform combinations of familiar written duple and triple tempo and meter beat patterns.

MT: a) teacher rates student-improvised rhythmic variations of a familiar written song. b) teacher rates student-written composition assignments. c) teacher rates students' performances of compositions.

18.   understand the theoretical basis for metric function of duple and triple tempo and meter beat patterns.

MT: student takes written test on knowledge of meter signatures and note value proportionalities.

Instrument Techniques Objectives

The technical aspects of playing an instrument are controlled by the demands of the musical objectives. Instrument technique results from studying and performing music. Learning techniques outside a musical context is a questionable practice. The objectives in the following lists have no particular sequeunce for learning but are, for the most part, all in effect from the first lesson and continue throughout instruction. The specifics for each objective depend upon the musical demands.

Accomplishment of instrument techniques is measured primarily through direct visual and aural observations by the teacher, student, or other students. The content of most technique objectives does not lend itself well to continuum ratings. The decision to be made in most cases is satisfactory or unsatisfactory performance. For this reason, the lists of objectives below do not include a measurement technique for each objective. The measurement technique for all objectives is the same: the teacher observes and rates instrument technique as satisfactory or unsatisfactory.

Technique Objectives for All Instruments

Students will be able to perform:
1.   with correct finger and hand positions.
2.   with acceptable body posture.
3.   with acceptable and characteristic tone quality.
4.   with acceptable intonation.
5.   effective tuning procedures for the instrument.

Technique Objectives for Wind Instruments

Students will be able to perform:
1.   correct assembly procedures for the instrument.
2.   with correct holding and support of the instrument.
3.   with correct embouchure formation.
4.   with effective breath support.
5.   tongue movements for various articulations.

6.   with controlled and accurate finger technique.
7.   with controlled and pleasing vibrato.

Technique Objectives for Stringed Instruments

Students will be able to perform:
1.   with correct holding and support of the instrument.
2.   various bowing techniques.
3.   pizzicato technique.
4.   with controlled and accurate finger technique.
5.   various left hand techniques—shifting, double stops, vibrato.

Technique Objectives for Percussion Instruments

Students will be able to perform:
1.   with appropriate instrument heights and positions.
2.   with correct stick and mallet handholds.
3.   on appropriate striking locations of instruments.
4.   with controlled stick technique—single taps, double bounce, multiple bounce.
5.   with controlled mallet technique.

Using Standardized Music Tests

Published standardized tests of music achievement and aptitude are important measurement tools for instrumental music. Unlike teacher-made tests and rating scales, published tests include established norm tables and are standardized with regard to administration and scoring. They afford the advantages of high quality, well-constructed test materials and comparisons of students' scores with norm groups. Most tests have machine scorable answer sheets which may be scored by hand or by computer optical scanning. Most tests can be administered to groups of students. The best source of information about a test is the test manual, which should include extensive explanation of the test content, administration, scoring procedures, norm groups, test reliability, test validity, and score interpretation.

During the past seventy years, a number of music achievement tests have been published in this country, most of them designed for school use. The most important consideration when choosing a published achievement test is whether the test content fits your content objectives. Published achievement test content often becomes dated with time and so earlier tests are no longer available. Achievement tests are most useful to measure long-term objectives, usually once or twice per school year. Score comparisons to national norms may be made, and equally important, local norms may be established over years of repeated testing. It is best, however, not to use scores obtained from published tests for determining music grades.

A number of music aptitude tests have also been published since the turn of the century in this country. Aptitude testing has undergone many changes as testing technology and the understanding of aptitude have evolved. Music aptitude may be defined as the potential to achieve musically. Many variables constitute music aptitude, but there is considerable research evidence that three of the main components are tonal, rhythmic, and musical sensitivity. Music aptitude tests should not require previous formal music training in order to take the tests. A number of tests published as aptitude tests are mainly achievement tests because the student must have musical training before taking the test.

Aptitude testing is especially important before beginning students on instruments. A reliable and valid aptitude test aids in identifying students who may achieve musically and in diagnosing musical strengths and weaknesses. Teaching efficiency and student success are directly affected. Aptitude tests should never be used as selection tools to decide who may or may not receive instrumental instruction.

Four common misconceptions exist about music aptitude testing and its relationship to beginning instrumentalists. The first is that student interest in starting instrumental instruction is a measure of aptitude. Research by Edwin Gordon and others has shown little or no relationship between interest and aptitude.[1] Although interest may be a deciding factor to begin intrumental instruction, it never substitutes for the music aptitude necessary for long-term commitment and success with an instrument. The second misconception is that academic aptitude (I.Q. test scores) is a measure of music aptitude. Again, there is considerable research evidence, for example, William Young's study, that I.Q. test scores have only a slight relationship to music aptitude.[2] In short, I.Q. scores should never be used to select instrumental students. The third misconception about music aptitude testing is that the promotional materials distributed by instrument companies are aptitude tests. None of these materials have proven reliability or validity as aptitude tests. At best, they may be used to generate interest, but they are frequently misused in schools by well-intentioned instructors. The fourth and last point of error is that aptitude tests may be teacher-made. This is analogous to teachers developing I.Q. tests in their schools. The complexity of a psychometrically sound aptitude test is beyond the scope of teacher-construction; teacher-made achievement tests are appropriate, however.

Selected published music achievement and aptitude tests are described here on the basis of content, quality of the test construction, and appropriateness for use with instrumental students. It must be emphasized that no test has value if the teacher does not understand how to interpret the scores. Measurement texts such as those by Robert Thorndike and Elizabeth Hagen, or Robert Ebel should prove most helpful. [3]

Published Music Achievement Tests

Iowa Tests of Music Literacy (ITML) by Edwin Gordon, published by The Bureau of Educational Research and Service (1970), The University of Iowa, Iowa City, IA 52240.

ITML is a tape-recorded test in six levels of difficulty. Each level contains two main tests, Tonal Concepts and Rhythm Concepts. Each main test contains three subtests, Aural Perception (is what you hear major or minor, duple or triple, etc.?), Reading Recognition (is what you see what you hear?), and Notational Understanding (complete the notation to fit what you hear). Each level takes about ninety minutes to administer, but any of the six subtests may be given on separate occasions. The item content is originally composed melodic and rhythmic fragments performed on a synthesizer. The manual contains percentile norm tables for Levels 1-3 in grades 4-6, 7-9, and 10-12; and for levels 4-6 in grades 7-9 and 10-12. Answer sheets may be hand or machine scored.

ITML is appropriate for beginning through advanced instrumental students. A profile of tonal and rhythm achievement progress may be charted if appropriate levels of the test are administered once or twice per school year.

Music Achievement Tests 1-4 (MAT) by Richard Colwell (1969, 1970), published by MAT, Inc., School of Music, University of Illinois, Urbana, IL 61801.

MAT is a set of four tests, each available on a long-playing record. The content is related to general music basal series. The test content is not sequenced by difficulty levels and need not be administered in chronological order. Each test contains three or four separate parts: Test 1—Pitch Discrimination, Interval Discrimination, Meter Discrimination; Test 2—Major-Minor Mode Discrimination, Feeling for

Tonal Center, Auditory-Visual Discrimination; Test 3—Tonal Memory, Melody Recognition, Pitch Recognition, Instrument Recognition; Test 4—Musical Style, Auditory-Visual Discrimination, Chord Recognition, Cadence Recognition. Item content, for the most part, consists of excerpts from familiar tunes. Percentile and standard score norm tables are furnished for Test 1 and Test 2 for individual grades 4-8 and for high school students. Norms for Test 3 and Test 4 are available individually for grades 4-12. In addition, combined norms are included for grades 4-6, 7-9, and 10-12 for students with instrumental experience. Answer sheets may be hand or machine scored. Many of the test Parts may be used with instrumental students whenever content objectives coincide.

The Watkins-Farnum Performance Scale (WFPS), Forms A and B, by John Watkins and Stephen Farnum, published by Hal Leonard Music, Inc., Winona, MN (1954) and *The Farnum String Scale* by Stephen Farnum, published by Hal Leonard Music, Inc. (1969).

The WFPS and its later variation, The Farnum String Scale, are the only published attempts at performance testing. WFPS consists of fourteen etudes which are claimed to be of increasing difficulty. The same etudes are performed individually by all instruments except snare drum. While a student sightreads the etudes, the rater records errors of pitch, rhythm (incorrect durations, rests, holds, and pauses), tempo changes, expression, slurs, and repeats. Any one error per measure results in the loss of a point. The manual includes limited reliability and validity information. Reported norms are inadequate.

The WFPS is most usable as a performance rating when norms are developed locally for each instrument. It is not advisable to compare scores among different instruments or to use the results to award music grades.

Published Music Aptitude Tests

Musical Aptitude Profile (MAP) by Edwin Gordon published by Houghton Mifflin Company, Boston (1965).

MAP is a tape-recorded aptitude test with three main sections, each with subtests: Tonal Imagery—Melody, Harmony; Rhythm Imagery—Tempo, Meter; Musical Sensitivity—Phrasing, Balance, and Style. The test is designed for group administration to students in grades 4 through 12. Three fifty-minute periods are recommended to complete administration. No formal music achievement is required to take the test. Students need take the test only once in their school careers. The test manual includes directions for administering, scoring, and interpreting results. Separate norm tables are included for grades 4 through 12. Answer sheets may be hand or machine scored. MAP is the only music aptitude test developed to this date which has established predictive validity for instrumental music success. [4]

Primary Measures of Music Audiation (PMMA) by Edwin Gordon, published by G.I.A. Publications, Inc., Chicago (1979).

PMMA is a tape-recorded aptitude test in two parts, Tonal Concepts and Rhythm Concepts. The test is designed for repeated group testing of students in grades K-3. About forty minutes is needed to administer the test. No formal music training is needed to take the test. Item content consists of pairs of tonal and rhythm patterns which students are to determine as same or different. The manual contains information for administering, scoring, and interpreting the test. Percentile norms are included for each grade. Answer sheets must be hand scored. PMMA should be of particular interest to teachers of keyboard and stringed instruments for use with students younger than grade 4.

Recording Achievement Data

If musical and instrument technique objectives are systematically taught and measured, productive evaluation is possible. An interim step between the measurement and evaluation processes is recording and transforming the data into meaningful information. Scores from aural and visual observations in the forms of teacher-made tests or rating scales provide quantified evidence for use in achievement evaluation. The raw scores from the variety of achievement measurements should be carefully collected for each student. Record books may be purchased or each student may be assigned a page in a three-ring binder for entering achievement information. Teachers must regularly record data for each student after it is collected. The data may then be interpreted and used to assess progress and to assign grades.

Transforming, Combining, and Weighting Scores

One of the purposes of measuring music achievement is to obtain objective data in numerical form. Quantified information may be accumulated and appropriately interpreted over periods of time. Raw score achievement information for each student is typically summarized and interpreted at the end of grading periods. Checklist data of satisfactory or unsatisfactory achievement for stated objectives are easily interpreted. Certain precautions must be observed when combining raw score data from tests and rating scales in order for the final results to be meaningful and fair for each student.

Raw scores are uninterpretable unless they undergo transformations which allow comparisons and combinations. Some of the most common score transformations are:

1.　Scores are sometimes rank-ordered from highest to lowest and arbitrarily divided into segments which are assigned letter grades. This procedure introduces much subjectivity and loss of precision in the data.

2.　Scores may be converted to percentages of content correct on a given test. The percentages may then be converted to predetermined categories of letter grades. Each student is in effect measured against the predetermined percentage amount of test content answered correctly. Although this procedure is relatively easy to accomplish, the validity of the grade is based upon the assumption that the test items are truly representative of the domain of knowledge being tested and that the test is highly reliable, which, in practice, is seldom realized. For example, the real question becomes not student achievement but whether or not eighty percent of one particular test accurately represents grade C or "average" work.

3.　Another transformation is to rank order scores from highest to lowest and then to convert them to percentiles. A given percentile defines the percentage of individuals who took the test and scored at or below the particular score associated with the percentile. Receiving a score at the 55th percentile means that 55 percent of the students taking the test scored at or below that particular score. This is a normative transformation that compares each student to all others in the test group. Letter grades may be arbitrarily assigned to percentile groups after the tests are scored.

4.　Standard score transformations are the only type which retain the absolute differences between raw scores. They can be directly combined and proportionately weighted. Because they relate to the properties of the normal distribution curve, standard scores are inappropriate when used with highly skewed distributions and, often, with very small groups. There are a number of standard score transformations; one of the most useful for test data is the T-score transformation. T-scores convert a distribution of raw scores to a mean of fifty and a standard deviation of ten. T-scores are obtained by first calculating the mean and standard deviation for the score distribution. A raw score is then transformed to a T-score by a) subtracting the mean and dividing by the standard deviation, b) multiplying by ten, and c) adding fifty. T-scores from different tests and ratings may now be directly combined or proportionally weighted to obtain summary data for determining achievement levels and grades.

Remember, it is never appropriate simply to add raw scores together. It is beyond the scope of this chapter to elaborate further on correct procedures for transforming, combining, and weighting raw score achievement data; the reader should consult the measurement texts listed at the close of the chapter for additional information.

Reporting Instrumental Music Achievement

Results and interpretations of measurement data from instrumental music achievement need regular reporting procedures. It is important to report achievement results to students, parents, and administrators so that the extent to which objectives have been met is obvious to all concerned. Students gain perspective of their achievement level. Parents should become more aware of content objectives through reporting procedures. Administrators are able to assess program strengths and weaknesses through accurately reported data.

Many instrumental instructors are uncertain about exactly what or how to report evaluations. Marks should clearly reflect achievement levels defined by specific musical and instrument technique objectives. Achievement marks are not interpretable if such other information as attendance, attitude, and effort are mixed with achievement data. Report cards may include separate areas for attendance and subjective evaluations of classroom behavior and effort. Record-keeping is then simplified, and all data is easily interpreted and understood.

It is advisable to use a separate written form to report instrumental achievement in addition to the usual academic report card. The instrumental report card may then be tailored to the needs of the particular school system and program. Individual reports of instrumental achievement should be specific enough to reflect current levels of attainment accurately, but should not be so detailed that they are cumbersome for the instructor to complete.

A format for an instrumental music report is suggested in Figure 6.1. Specific tonal, rhythmic, and technical objectives taken from the lists earlier in this chapter would be included as needed in

Instrumental Music Report

Name_____   Grade_____

O = Outstanding   S = Satisfactory progress   N = Not measured this grade period
U = Unsatisfactory progress

Class Totals

	1	2	3	4
O				
S				
U				

Days Absent

1	2	3	4

1   2   3   4   Tonality Objectives
                     1.
                     2.
                     .
                     .
                     .

1   2   3   4   Rhythm Objectives
                     1.
                     2.
                     .
                     .
                     .

1   2   3   4   Technique Objectives
                     1.
                     2.
                     .
                     .

Parent's Signature   1._____

                     2._____

                     3._____

                     4._____

Fig. 6.1.   Model for an instrumental music report.

each section. Class totals for each grade are reported to allow meaningful comparisons. The report is designed for four grade periods of nine weeks each in a typical school year. More grade periods could be used.

Variations to consider with the format in 6.1 include:

1. Different letter designations may be used. Regardless of the number of letter marks used or what letters are chosen, it is essential that clear definitions of each category are listed on the report.

2. A separate section for behavior and attitude assessment may be added.

3. A separate section may be added to report Musical Aptitude Profile percentile rankings.

4. The back of the report or a separate sheet may be used to explain the content objectives further to parents.

5. A separate section may be added to list music knowledge objectives—terms, composers, forms, etc.

6. Effort may be reported for each objective by adding another column of boxes for grade periods and using the same letter designations.

7. Blank space for written comments by the instructor or by parents may be added.

Review Questions

1. What is the basis for evaluation of instrumental music achievement?

2. Why should regular measurement of objectives occur?

3. Why is it important to measure music achievement of individual students?

4. What place does visual observation have as a measurement tool?

5. How may subjectivity be controlled when constructing and using rating scales?

6. How might you measure students' ability to recognize minor tonic and dominant function tonal patterns in notation?

7. How might you measure students' ability to perform self-created combinations of familiar triple meter patterns?

8. How might you measure students' ability to form a correct embouchure?

9. What advantages do published standardized tests have over teacher-made tests?

10. For what purposes should music aptitude tests be administered?

11. How do achievement tests differ from aptitude tests?

For Further Reading

Colwell, Richard. *The Evaluation of Music Teaching and Learning.* Englewood Cliffs: Prentice-Hall, 1970.

Gordon, Edwin. *The Psychology of Music Teaching.* Englewood Cliffs: Prentice-Hall, 1971.

Gronlund, Norman E. *Measurement & Evaluation in Teaching* 3d ed. New York: Macmillan Co., 1976.

Lehman, Paul. *Tests and Measurements in Music.* Englewood Cliffs: Prentice-Hall, 1968.

APPENDIX A:
DIALOGUE TECHNIQUES

A DIALOGUE is basically a statement and response. A dialogue response answers the statement with a different or altered response whereas an echo technique response is an exact repetition of the statement.

Dialogue techniques are particularly useful in teaching a vocabulary of tonal and rhythm patterns. Many variations are possible, and many levels of difficulty may be established by altering the content and task. Content may be drilled with dialogue techniques, since students enjoy the process. The learning sequence level may be varied while the rhythm or tonal pattern content remains the same or pattern content may be varied while learning sequence level remains the same. Individual differences are easily managed because students can respond within their own vocabulary knowledge.

Dialogue techniques are especially effective as measurement techniques in which many students can individually demonstrate skill and knowledge in brief periods of time. Diagnosis of student achievement levels and skills is facilitated. For example, during a dialogue activity, the teacher discovers that a particular student can provide the correct rhythm syllables (VA) for a given clapped pattern but is unable to read the pattern. The student may recognize the written symbols but cannot read them accurately in rhythm. This indicates a need for more practice with the syllables (VA) before further reading of the pattern.

The first examples described below are for rhythm pattern dialogues. The statements (S) may be provided by the teacher or by a student leader. It is recommended that patterns be restricted to four tempo beats for each statement and response. Three forms of response (R) are included—clapping, chanting (with correct rhythm syllables), or playing.

1. (S) Clap patterns   (Aural/Oral recall or creativity)
   (R) Clap/play different patterns   (A/O recall or creativity)
2. (S) Clap patterns   (A/O recall or creativity)
   (R) Chants same pattern   (VA)
3. (S) Chants patterns   (VA creativity—unless pattern is read, then SA)
   (R) Claps/plays different patterns   (A/O creativity)
4. (S) Chants patterns   (VA creativity or SA if read)
   (R) Chants different patterns   (VA creativity)

The task difficulty of the preceding rhythm dialogues may be increased by: 1) alternating duple with triple meter statement and responses; 2) using unusual meter patterns; 3) alternating duple or triple meter with unusual meter statements and responses; 4) using different patterns on each of the four tempo beats within a statement and response, thus increasing the memory task; 5) increasing the number of sounds per pattern; 6) including patterns with ties and elongations across tempo beats; and 7) stressing less familiar or more recently learned patterns. The teacher must take care that difficulty levels do not frustrate students.

Similarly, tonal patterns may be drilled with dialogue techniques. Tonal pattern dialogues should avoid rhythmic interaction and normally consist of two to five pitches in each statement and response. Patterns should relate to tonic function major and minor initially and then to dominant and subdominant chords before becoming more complex, either by relating to lesser-used chords or to more than one chord in a pattern. Examples of tonal pattern dialogue formats are:

1. (S) Sing pattern on neutral syllable (loo) (A/O recall or creativity)
   (R) Sing a different pattern with neutral syllable (A/O recall or creativity)
2. (S) Sing pattern on neutral syllable (loo) (A/O recall or creativity)
   (R) Sing same pattern with syllables (VA)
3. (S) Sing pattern with syllables (VA or if read, SA)
   (R) Sing different patterns with syllables (VA creativity)

4. (S) Sing pattern on neutral syllable (loo) (A/O recall or creativity)
    (R) Play a different pattern (A/O recall or creativity)
5. (S) Play pattern (A/O recall or creativity)
    (R) Sing same pattern with syllables (VA), then play it (A/O)
6. (S) Play pattern (A/O recall or creativity)
    (R) Play a different pattern (A/O recall or creativity)

APPENDIX B:
SONGS CATEGORIZED BY RANGE

Range of do-mi:
At Pierrot's Door (no B section)
Hot Cross Buns
Mary Had a Little Lamb (change *sol* to *mi*)

Range of do-sol:
Deaf Woman's Courtship
Go Tell Aunt Rhody
 ingle Bells (chorus)
Lightly Row
O Come Little Children
Oats, Peas, Beans
Ode to Joy Theme (Beethoven's 9th Symphony)
Going Home Theme (Dvorak's "New World" Symphony)
When Day Is Done
When the Saints Go Marching In

Range of la-mi:
Hey, Ho, Nobody Home (round)

Range of do-la:
A Tisket, A Tasket
Baa, Baa, Black Sheep
For He's A Jolly Good Fellow
Hickory Dickory Dock
Kum Ba Ya
London Bridge

Lovely Evening (round)
Michael, Row the Boat Ashore
Oh, Susanna
Old Time Religion
Rock-a My Soul
This Old Man
Twinkle, Twinkle Little Star
Up on the Housetop
Way Down Yonder in the Pawpaw Patch

Range of sol-mi:
Jolly Old St. Nicholas
Little Brown Church in the Valley
Old MacDonald
Tom Dooley

Range of sol-fa:
Aura Lee
Bingo

Range of do-do:
Camptown Races
Deck the Halls
Drink to Me Only
Hail, Hail, The Gang's All Here
Kookaburra (round)
Little Tom Tinker
Marines Hymn
Oh Dear, What Can the Matter Be
On Top of Old Smoky
Over the River and through the Woods
Ring, Ring the Banjo
Row, Row, Row Your Boat
The First Noel
Three Blind Mice

Range of sol-sol:
Amazing Grace
Are You Sleeping?
Clementine (chorus)
Down in the Valley
Home on the Range
Let Us Sing Together (round)
Long, Long Ago

Oh Tannenbaum
Old Hundredth (The Doxology)

Range of mi-mi:
My Bonnie
When Johnny Comes Marching Home

APPENDIX C:
CONDUCTING PATTERNS
AND METER SIGNATURES

RHYTHMIC feeling should be conveyed visually through conducting patterns in large group rehearsals and performances. It is the conductor's responsibility to correlate the beat pattern with the underlying feeling and inform the performers of the desired effect. Confusion may occur when the same beat patterns are used indiscriminately to indicate tempo beat feeling and meter beat feeling.

Three basic beat patterns are used for conducting rhythmic feeling:

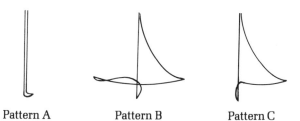

Pattern A   Pattern B   Pattern C

Whenever Pattern A is used it indicates two *tempo* beats per measure and is normally used with music written with meter signatures of two-quarter ($\frac{2}{4}$), two-half ($\frac{2}{2}$), two-eighth ($\frac{2}{8}$), and six-eighth ($\frac{6}{8}$). It is also used for meter signatures with 5 as the upper number to indicate the two uneven tempo beats. Many songs are written with a 4 as the upper meter signature number but are actually felt as two tempo beats per measure as in alla breve (₵). Pattern A is appropriate for any music which is felt in two tempo beats per measure regardless of the meter signature. Note that this same beat pattern may be used for music in duple, triple, or unusual meter feeling. The music will be visually grouped in two tempo beats per measure according to whatever note values are assigned the tempo beat feeling.

Pattern B is used to indicate four *tempo* beats per measure. It is normally employed with music written in four-quarter ($\frac{4}{4}$), four-half ($\frac{4}{2}$), four-eighth ($\frac{4}{8}$), and twelve-eighth ($\frac{12}{8}$). It is also used with ($\frac{9}{8}$) when it represents unusual meter with four tempo beats per measure. It is also possible (although usually confusing) to use Pattern B to indicate duple meter beat feeling in music written with two tempo beats per measure. Again, notice that the same beat pattern may be used for music in duple, triple, or unusual meter feeling. Visual representation of the number of tempo beats felt per measure determines the correct beat pattern.

Pattern C is commonly used and is appropriate for indicating three *meter* beats per measure in three-half ($\frac{3}{2}$), three-quarter ($\frac{3}{4}$), and three-eighth ($\frac{3}{8}$) whenever the music is felt with one tempo beat per measure. Music written with three as the top meter signature number and felt as one tempo beat per measure can also be conducted with rhythmic flow by using Pattern A for every two measures. Pattern C may also be used to indicate three *tempo* beats per measure in music with meter signatures of three-half ($\frac{3}{2}$), three-quarter ($\frac{3}{4}$), three-eighth ($\frac{3}{8}$), and nine-eighth ($\frac{9}{8}$). Special care must be taken when using Pattern C always to inform the performers whether tempo or meter beat feeling is indicated by the beat pattern.

APPENDIX D:
TRIPLE METER SONGS

THE FOLLOWING list of fifty song titles is representative of many of
the available melodies mainly from folk music which have an
underlying triple meter feeling (pat-clap-clap).

Amazing Grace
The Ash Grove
The Band Played On
Barbara Allen
Blow the Man Down
Campbells Are Comin'
Daisy, Daisy
Dona Nobis Pacem (round)
Down in the Valley
Drink to Me Only
Eency Weency Spider
The Farmer in the Dell
The First Noel
Flow Gently Sweet Afton
Goober Peas
Goodbye, Old Paint
Hey Diddle Diddle
Hickory, Dickory, Dock
Hole in the Bucket
Home on the Range
In the Good Old Summertime
Kum Ba Ya

Lavender's Blue
Little Jack Horner
Little Tom Tinker
Looby Loo
The Man on the Flying Trapeze
The Mulberry Bush
My Bonnie
Oats, Peas, Beans
Oh Dear, What Can the Matter Be?
Oh, How Lovely Is the Evening (round)
On Top of Old Smoky
Over the River and through the Woods
Pop Goes the Weasel
Ring around the Rosy
Row, Row, Row Your Boat
Sailing, Sailing
Scarborough Fair
Silent Night
So Long, It's Been Good to Know You
Streets of Laredo
Summer Is A-Comin' In (round)
Sweet and Low
Sweet Betsy from Pike
Vive La Compagnie
We Gather Together
We Three Kings of Orient Are
When Johnny Comes Marching Home
Whoopee Ti Yi Yo

NOTES

Chapter 1

1.   Edward Bailey Birge, *History of Public School Music in the United States* (New and Augmented Edition), (Washington, D.C.: Music Educators' National Conference, 1966).

2.   Quoted in Carol Bryant, *And the Band Played On* (Washington, D.C.: Smithsonian Institution Press, 1975), p. 21.

3.   Albert Mitchell, *Class Method for Violin* (Boston: Oliver Ditson Co., 1924).

4.   Benjamin Stuber, *Instrumental Music Course* (Chicago: E. T. Root & Sons, 1923).

5.   Joseph Maddy and Thaddeus Giddings, *The Universal Teacher* (Elkhart: C. G. Conn, 1923, 1926, Cincinnati: The Willis Music Co.).

6.   Theodore Normann, *Instrumental Music in the Public Schools* (Philadelphia: Oliver Ditson Co., 1941), pp. 142-44.

7.   *Rubank Elementary Method* (Miami: Rubank, Inc. 1934).

8.   Claude Smith, Paul Yoder, and Harold Bachman, *Smith-Yoder-Bachman Ensemble Band Method* (Park Ridge: Neil A. Kjos Music Co., 1939).

9.   Charles Peters and Matt Betton, *Take One* (Park Ridge: Neil A. Kjos Music Co., 1972).

10.   James O. Froseth, *The Individualized Instructor* (Chicago: G.I.A. Publications, Inc., 1970).

11.   Guy Kinney, *Complete Guide to Teaching Small Instrumental Groups in the High School* (West Nyack: Parker Publishing Co., 1981).

12.   James O. Froseth, *NABIM Recruiting Manual* (Chicago: G.I.A. Publications, Inc., 1974).

13.   Raymond Roth, "Don't They Also Love Music?" *The Instrumentalist* 36, no. 5 (December, 1981): 110, 102-3.

14.   Lyle C. Merriman, *Woodwind Research Guide* (Evanston: The Instrumentalist Co., 1978).

15.   Charles H. Benner, *Teaching Performing Groups* (Washington, D.C.: Music Educators' National Conference, 1972); George L. Duerksen, *Teaching Instrumental Music* (Washington, D.C.: Music Educators' National Conference, 1972).

Chapter 2

1.   Louis P. Thorpe, "Learning Theory and Music Teaching" in *Basic Concepts in Music Education, The Fifty-seventh Yearbook of the National Society for the Study of Education* (Part I), ed. Nelson B. Henry (Chicago: Univ. of Chicago Press, 1958), p. 163.

2.   James L. Mursell and Mabelle Glenn, *The Psychology of School Music Teaching* (New York: Silver Burdett Co., 1931), p. 1.

3.   James L. Mursell, "Growth Processes in Music Education," in *Basic Concepts in Music Education, The Fifty-seventh Yearbook of the National Society for the Study of Education* (Part I), ed. Nelson B. Henry (Chicago: Univ. of Chicago Press, 1958), p. 153.

4.   Ibid., p. 157.

5.   Jerome S. Bruner, *The Process of Education* (Cambridge: Harvard Univ. Press, 1960).

6.   Ibid., p. 31.

7.   Ibid., p. 12.

8.   Jerome S. Bruner, *Toward a Theory of Instruction* (Cambridge: Harvard Univ. Press, 1966); ibid., p. 49.

9.   Robert M. Gagne, *The Conditions of Learning* (New York: Holt, Rinehart and Winston, 1965).

10.   Edwin Gordon, *The Psychology of Music Teaching* (Englewood Cliffs: Prentice-Hall, 1971).

11.   Robert Sidnell, *Building Instructional Programs in Music Education* (Englewood Cliffs: Prentice-Hall, 1973).

12.   Benjamin S. Bloom and Lauren A. Sosniak, "Talent Development vs. Schooling," *Educational Leadership* (November, 1981): 90.

13.   Ibid., p. 90.

14.   Will S. Monroe, *History of the Pestalozzian Movement in the United States* (Syracuse: C. W. Bardeen, 1907), p. 145, quoted in Charles Leonhard and Robert House, *Foundations and Principles of*

Music Education (New York: McGraw-Hill, 1959), pp. 52-53.

15. Emil A. Holz and Roger E. Jacobi, *Teaching Band Instruments to Beginners* (Englewood Cliffs: Prentice-Hall, 1966), pp. 46-50.

16. *Documentary Report of the Ann Arbor Symposium* (Reston, VA: Music Educators National Conference, 1981).

17. Edwin E. Gordon, *Learning Sequences in Music* (Chicago: G.I.A. Publications, Inc., 1980).

18. Barry L. Velleman, "Speaking of Jazz," *Music Educators Journal*, 65, no. 2 (October, 1978): 28-31.

Chapter 3

1. Robert W. Lundin, *An Objective Psychology of Music*, 2d ed. (New York: Ronald Press, 1967). See also Paul R. Farnsworth, *The Social Psychology of Music*, 2d ed. (Ames: Iowa State Univ. Press, 1969).

2. Jack A. Taylor, "Perception of Tonality in Short Melodies," *Journal of Research in Music Education*, 24, no. 4 (1976): 197-208.

3. Leonard Meyer, *Emotion and Meaning in Music* (Chicago: Univ. of Chicago Press, 1956); and Meyer, *Music, the Arts, and Ideas* (Chicago: Univ. of Chicago Press, 1967).

4. Robert Nye, *Music in the Elementary School*, 4th ed. (Englewood Cliffs: Prentice-Hall, Inc., 1977), chapter 12, and Edwin Gordon, *The Psychology of Music Teaching* (Englewood Cliffs: Prentice-Hall, 1971), chapter 6.

5. Thomas John Harris, "An Investigation of the Effectiveness of an Intonation Training Program upon Junior and Senior High School Wind Instrumentalists," Ed.D. diss., University of Illinois, 1977.

6. Robert J. McGarry, "A Teaching Experience to Measure the Extent to Which Vocalization Contributes to the Development of Selected Instrumental Music Performance Skills," Ed.D. diss., New York University, 1967.

7. Charles A. Elliott, "The Effect of Vocalization Upon the Sense of Pitch of the Students in Selected Beginning Band Classes," *Journal of Research in Music Education*, 20, no. 4 (Winter, 1972): 496-500; William F. Schlacks, "The Effect of Vocalization Through an Interval Training Program Upon the Pitch Accuracy of High School Band Students," Ph.D. diss., University of Miami, 1981.

8. Shinichi Suzuki, *Nurtured by Love* (New York: Exposition Press, 1969).

9. John Sperti, "Adaptation of Certain Aspects of the Suzuki Method to the Teaching of the Clarinet: An Experimental Investigation Testing the Comparative Effectiveness of Two Different Pedagogical Methodologies," Ed.D. diss., New York Univ., 1970.

10. Carol B. MacKnight, "The Effects of Tonal Pattern Training on the Performance Achievement of Beginning Wind Instrumentalists," *Experimental Research in the Psychology of Music: Studies in the Psychology of Music* 10 (1975): 53-76.

11. Edwin E. Gordon, *Learning Sequences in Music* (Chicago: G.I.A. Publications, Inc., 1980).

12. Peter W. Dykema and Hannah M. Cundiff, *School Music Handbook* (Boston: C. C. Birchard & Co., 1955), p. 70.

Chapter 4

1. James L. Mursell and Mabelle Glenn, *The Psychology of School Music Teaching* (New York: Silver Burdett Co., 1931), p. 311.

2. Emile-Jacques Dalcroze, *Rhythm, Music & Education*, trans. H. Rubenstein, rev. ed. of 1921 version (Redcourt, England: The Dalcroze Society, Inc., 1967), p. 36.

3. Edwin Gordon, *The Psychology of Music Teaching* (Englewood Cliffs: Prentice-Hall, 1971), p. 67.

4. Emile-Jacques Dalcroze, *Rhythm, Music & Education*.

5. Gordon, *The Psychology of Music Teaching*. Allen I. McHose and Ruth N. Tibbs, *Sight-Singing Manual* (New York: Appleton-Century-Crofts, 1945).

6. Edgar E. Dittemore, "An Investigation of Some Musical Capabilities of Elementary School Children," *Experimental Research in the Psychology of Music: Studies in the Psychology of Music*, 6 (1970): 1-44. Robert DeYarman, "An Experimental Analysis of the Development of Rhythmic and Tonal Capabilities of Kindergarten and First Grade Children," *Experimental Research in the Psychology of Music: Studies in the Psychology of Music* 10 (1975): 1-23. Mary Palmer, "Relative Effectiveness of Two Approaches to Rhythm Reading for Fourth-Grade Students," *Journal of Research in Music Education* 24 (1976): 110-18.

7. Nilo Hovey, *Efficient Rehearsal Procedures for School Bands* (Elkhart: The Selmer Co., 1976), p. 52.

Chapter 5

1. James L. Mursell and Mabelle Glenn, *The Psychology of School Music Teaching* (New York: Silver Burdett Co., 1931), p. 302.
2. Frank R. Wilson, *Mind, Muscle and Music: Physiological Clues to Better Teaching*, Teachercraft Bulletin, No. 4, (Elkhart: The Selmer Co., 1981), p. 14.
3. Nilo Hovey, *Efficient Rehearsal Procedures for School Bands* (Elkhart: The Selmer Co., 1976).

Chapter 6

1. Edwin Gordon, *A Three-Year Longitudinal Predictive Validity Study of the Musical Aptitude Profile* (Iowa City: Univ. of Iowa Press, 1967).
2. William T. Young, "The Role of Musical Aptitude, Intelligence, and Academic Achievement in Predicting the Musical Attainment of Elementary Instrumental Students," *Journal of Research in Music Education* 19 (1971): 385-98.
3. Robert L. Thorndike and Elizabeth Hagen, *Measurement and Evaluation in Psychology and Education*, 4th ed. (New York: John Wiley and Sons, 1977). Robert L. Ebel, *Essentials of Educational Measurement*, 3d ed. (Englewood Cliffs: Prentice-Hall, 1979).
4. Gordon, *A Three-Year Longitudinal Predictive Study*, p. 35.

INDEX